Playing, Laughing and Learning with Children on the Autism Spectrum

of related interest

My Social Story Book
Carol Gray and Abbie Leigh White
Illustrated by Sean McAndrew
ISBN 1 85302 950 5

Relationship Development Intervention with Young Children
Social and Emotional Development Activities for Asperger Syndrome, Autism, PDD and NLD
Steven E. Gutstein and Rachelle K. Sheely
ISBN 1 84310 714 7

Caring for a Child with Autism
A Practical Guide for Parents
Martine Ives and Nell Munro, National Autistic Society
ISBN 1 85302 996 3

Asperger's Syndrome
A Guide for Parents and Professionals
Tony Attwood
Foreword by Lorna Wing
ISBN 1 85302 577 1

Autism and Play
Jannik Beyer and Lone Gammeltoft
ISBN 1 85302 845 2

Giggle Time – Establishing the Social Connection
A Program to Develop the Communication Skills of Children with Autism
Susan Aud Sonders
ISBN 1 84310 716 3

Playing, Laughing and Learning with Children on the Autism Spectrum

A Practical Resource of Play Ideas for Parents and Carers

Julia Moor

Jessica Kingsley Publishers
London and Philadelphia

First published in the United Kingdom in 2002
by Jessica Kingsley Publishers
116 Pentonville Road
London N1 9JB, UK
and
400 Market Street, Suite 400
Philadelphia, PA 19106, USA

www.jkp.com

Copyright © Julia Moor 2002
Second impression 2003
Third impression 2004
Reprinted twice in 2005
Sixth impression 2006

Library of Congress Cataloging in Publication Data

Moor, Julia, 1966–
   Playing, laughing, and learning with children on the autism spectrum : a practical resource of play ideas for parents and carers / Julia Moor.
      p. Cm.
   Includes bibliographical references and index.
   ISBN 1-84310-060-6 (alk paper)
   1. Autistic children--Treatment. 2. Autism in children--Treatment. 3. Play therapy. 4. Parent and child. I. Title.

RJ506.A9 M66 2002
6168.92'8982065153--dc21

                                                                                    2002021521

British Library Cataloguing in Publication Data
A CIP catalogue record for this book is available from the British Library

ISBN-13: 978 1 84310 060 7
ISBN-10: 1 84310 060 6

Printed and Bound in Great Britain by
Athenaeum Press, Gateshead, Tyne and We

Contents

Acknowledgements

With thanks to the members of the Leeds and District ABC Group (Autism, Behaviour and Communication) who completed my survey and shared their valuable ideas and experiences.

Thanks also to Joanne Sandiford, Specialist Speech and Language Therapist, and Terence Gaussen, Consultant Clinical Psychologist – (Belmont House Child Development Team Leeds), for their time and comments in the production of this book, and for their invaluable input post-diagnosis to our son's (and our own!) early learning.

Thanks finally to the adults with learning difficulties who attend my art groups and have taught me as much about their thoughts, feelings and experiences as I have taught them about creativity.

*To my husband Chris,
for his loving support and dedication
and for being with me on the journey
every step of the way.*

Introduction

When our son was diagnosed with an *autistic spectrum disorder* at the age of two and a half, like thousands of parents before us we roller-coasted through the typical emotional responses: dismay, grief, fear for our future, but finally relief. We conclusively had a name for this condition that was filling our little boy's life with distress, impossible, repetitive and meaningless routines and such a reluctance to respond to us that we were sure he was deaf.

At the age of two, the world and people around Robin were mainly there to be avoided. His focus was only on 'parts' with no motivation to seek out the meaning of the 'whole': wheels on cars; strings on pull-along toys; lids on containers. Direct intervention, overly enthusiastic voices and physical encouragement to 'play properly' were met with hysterical screaming.

When we were given the diagnosis, upsetting as it was, it felt like we'd been given a map to not quite get out of the maze but at least to understand where we were in it.

As well as dealing with the challenges of obsessional behaviour, inflexibility, anxiety and frustration, my biggest concern was how to engage my son in meaningful activities at home – how do *I* help him *play*? At the time, there was lots of information available on autism, there was help with his speech and behaviour and health, but I simply found very little on how to play with my son – what to fill his hours with. Having studied child development in the past, coupled with my gut instinct as a Mum, I knew that he

was missing a vital part of his childhood and watching his mean-
ingless rituals and being constantly shut out were breaking my
heart.

For 12 months my main focus had been getting through the
day without distress, but I wanted more than this for my son and
felt angry with the autism for robbing him of what I felt was his
birthright. It seemed that so many things were off limits; his world
(and mine) was getting smaller and smaller; at an age when curiosity was meant to urge him forward – to explore, to communicate,
to experience and understand his world – my son simply wanted
to shut it out. Frustratingly for me I knew that there was vast
potential; an able, intelligent little boy held hostage by the different way in which his brain thinks and processes.

As someone who likes to feel there is a practical solution to
everything, I decided to haul myself out of the pit of 'why us?' and
to really try to understand first, his disorder and second, how he as
an *individual* expressed his autism. Armed with this information I
knew there'd be no miracles but at least I'd be making informed
choices and be doing everything in my power to shorten the
distance between his world and mine. On top of this I just felt I
had to find a constructive way to fill what seemed to be an eternity
of weeks and months with a little boy that simply didn't want to
engage with the planet he was born on. I didn't know him.

I began to realize that the direct 'front door' approach to interaction was useless: "look at this", "Let's do this" "Come here and
see" – they were cues for him to protest or run off and avoid interaction; *fight or flight*. Instinctively I felt there must be other
pathways to access my son, and what I found through trial and
error was that there was indeed a 'back door' where I could sneak
in and capture his attention without him even realizing that was
what I was doing!

Gradually over two years we built up a repertoire of play, transferring similar indirect techniques from one activity to the next, building on success and learning from failure. I discovered how to improve communication, how to structure not only the day as a series of activities but activities as a series of tasks. I also found I could punctuate the day with short bursts of direct learning tolerated by the prospect of a variety of motivational strategies.

It dawned on me through talking to and reading about other parents that they too had similar methods. After surveying a hundred such parents it became apparent that there were ideas out there but that there was also desperation for more. Our children are very individual; they deal with their autism in unique ways and are affected to different degrees with varying associated learning difficulties. Yet there are so many common threads: a need for routine and visual cues, problems with sensory overload, and a natural motivation to avoid anything outside the repertoire of familiarity.

Four years ago I needed a book of ideas; something that related to my son's specific collection of problems. Everything I assumed about parenting – providing love, attention and a stimulating environment – was rewritten by his diagnosis. It stripped me of my confidence as a mum. I questioned common sense because even that often didn't work. Yet this book is about common sense. Mums and dads are in a prime position to help their children reach their fullest potential. Parents come armed with unconditional love, an unsurpassed knowledge of their individual child and the motivation and commitment to do 'whatever it takes'. I hope this book will not only provide you with a collection of useful ideas but will help you find a way of playing with your child that rebuilds confidence and relationships. The ideas are there to dip in and try. Some may work, some may not – they do not constitute a task list that has to be ticked off and worked through! Choose those that you feel your child is *ready* to tackle, and that you are confident trying; leave the rest for weeks, months or even years later.

Our children's development doesn't correspond to a set of ages and stages and as such there are no age guidelines. Keep moving forward by carefully monitoring what your child is capable of and ready to tackle next – but don't rush, push or pitch your expectations in advance of his ability. More fundamentally, the point is to illustrate that by really *observing* and *understanding* your child you can learn to tune into his most receptive moments, to tailor the environment to increase these opportunities and to interact with him in a manner that prolongs them.

So what qualifies me to put these ideas together? It isn't my recent degree in psychology or my eight years working with adults with learning disabilities (many of whom have autism); it is being a mum to a little boy who has challenged me all his waking (and sleeping!) hours, day in and day out, to understand the way his brain works and the way he as an individual thinks, and to use this information to help him play, both independently, and to engage with me in a variety of shared activities. I would not dare to portray myself as an expert on autism, but living with and loving a child with autism is an incredible journey of learning and re-evaluating what we expect from parenthood. As parents we often feel helpless when our children are first diagnosed – yet as parents we are in the best possible position to help.

Please note that the individual examples in the book are illustrations based on the types of experience reported back to me in the surveys and on my own experience. I've used the male gender throughout – this is simply to make reading easier and less formal. Throughout the book there are several comparisons to 'non-autistic' children. I prefer this term to the ambiguous word 'normal'.

Chapter 1

Why is Playing So Important?

Think about your childhood – your earliest memories of how you filled your time. You probably think you weren't doing anything in particular, just messing about with toys and friends, but what you were doing in fact was *developing* and preparing for adulthood in a most miraculous way. Play and social development go hand in hand – one is a vehicle for the other. Underpinning play is *interaction* – from the instinctive imitative gestures and early interactions between babies and their care givers, to the complex fantasy play of school children. As the child develops through this interactive play, he is forming a sense of who he is – his own identity – and his social awareness grows as he begins to understand that perspectives other than his own exist. He learns social skills such as co-operation, empathy and respect.

Social development is just one consequence of being able to play. Playing is also a useful way to:

- develop 'symbolic understanding' – to understand that toy objects can represent real ones. Being able to use symbols in this way enables children to learn about the real world and how to interact with their environment, and puts in place the structures necessary for language

- test how material objects work and how actions can change outcomes, for example 'If I lift this ramp up, the toy car slides down' or 'What happens if I pour water from this beaker into this little cup?'

- try out frightening ideas safely, for example 'The bad wolf is hiding and he's going to get me if I make a noise…'

- work out the relations between people and how to behave and what to expect in certain situations, for example playing doctors, families, teachers

- express imagination and creativity through music, dancing, drawing, playdough etc., giving the child a sense of esteem and pride in his achievements

- re-enact everyday situations using toys and apply different storylines and consequences for example 'Mummy and little girl are out walking, oh no little girl has fallen…lets get a plaster…' or '…call an ambulance…'or '… kiss it better…' etc.

This list of why play is important is not definitive and obviously the child is completely unaware as to why he is playing – he just wants to. Instinctively he is motivated to initiate interaction with people and with his environment, and the nice feeling he gets from doing it stimulates him to keep doing it.

Why is play so difficult for children with autism?

First look at the problems common (in varying degrees) to *all* children on the autism spectrum:

- *Language* problems both in expressing and understanding the content of speech.

- Problems with *social interaction* – an unwillingness to allow others to share experiences, a lack of understanding of the thoughts and feelings and intentions of others and a general problem with the interpretation of non-verbal cues: facial expressions, tone of voice etc.

- Problems of *imagination* – difficulty in grasping the meaning of imaginary situations, often leading to repetitive, obsessive actions that only mean something to the child himself.

Given that each of the above is an essential ingredient that allows children to play, it's no wonder the child with autism feels lost and confused and resorts to activities that are meaningful and comforting only to him, even if they are repetitive and inappropriate.

So what do we actually mean by play?

The first thing that springs to mind when we mention play is the use of toys. This can be misleading – abandon a non-autistic three-year-old in a room filled with unfamiliar toys and he will flit from one to the other, not really knowing what to do with them; he needs interaction with an adult – to be shown and helped so that later he can share the experience with another child. Often the interaction is more rewarding to the child than the toy itself; he delights in the adult's delight at an object. In fact the adult's reactions teach him how to react, which he can then generalize to a new type of a familiar toy.

The key to playing is therefore *interaction*. 'But this is so difficult with my youngster', I hear you say. It certainly is, especially if your child simply doesn't understand that communication 'means' anything. The extent and quality of your interactions will differ according to your individual child's level of disability but the effort (and you will need lots of it!) will be rewarding both to you and your child as you begin to build structures for learning and communicating in the future. Toys are tools or props to aid inter-action through play, often the minimum or even no props are needed; a box, a cushion, a ball or you may adapt a game/toy that you already have.

Putting these ideas together hopefully illustrates that although teaching your child how to *behave* and *respond* in certain situations is useful, developing in him a real sense of enjoyment in interac-tion will further motivate him to seek out interaction (probably against the better judgement of his autistic brain) and allow him to socially develop to the best of his potential.

Using this book

Try to read Chapters 2, 3 and 4 to start off with. These chapters look at the general principles of using indirect non-confron-tational play approaches with short bursts of structured directed play. They give you ideas of how to set about finding different pathways to access your child's attention and how to create oppor-tunities for him to interact and communicate, as well as tackling the practicalities of using and organizing the play equipment you already have. The rest of the chapters look at specific areas of play and are filled with practical ideas for how to approach them and maximise interaction opportunities and learning potential. Not all the play ideas will be appropriate for your child. Some are pitched at 'difficult to reach' children who may have additional learning difficulties; others are suitable for verbal, able children needing on-going activities. Choose those suited to *your* child and the areas that you feel need to be worked on.

Chapter 2

Early Playing Skills: Gaining Attention and Sharing Space

What does sharing space mean?

It means your joint attention is fixed on the same thing at the same time, both of you are probably experiencing the same reaction and both of you are aware that the other is involved. With non-autistic children this happens so naturally and so frequently that parent and child are oblivious to it without the need for analysis! As parents of children with autism we need to be aware of the processes at work so that, to begin with, we can consciously create a sense of shared space. 'Sharing space' is not simply about sharing the same physical experience, it's about sharing attention, emotion and understanding, all of which are critical to early communication.

The drive to avoid

In contrast to their peers, young children with autism are actually motivated to *avoid* 'sharing space', to resist the discomfort that attempts at eye contact, physical contact and interaction from others can cause. Consequently they also avoid learning the *benefits* that communication brings or indeed learning that communication actually 'means' something to them. Through deliberate attempts to encourage your child to fleetingly share his attention you can move *beyond* his initial aversion to show him that communication is actually a good thing. Being able to communicate (in which ever way he can) will enable him to express his needs and emotions and understand the people and world around him in a way that can actually lessen his anxiety in the long run. Always be aware of the anxiety and discomfort that direct approaches to interact with your child may be causing. Let your understanding of these feelings be reflected in gentle non-invasive interactions and where a direct approach is used, keep it to short comfortable bursts.

How do you try to 'share space' with a child with autism?

Before you can attempt to interact with your child at a level that might be called joint play, you need to bring about a realization in him that no matter how uncomfortable the feelings are, to *share your space* even for a few seconds is such fun and brings such benefits that it can override his drive to shut you out.

When parents become aware that their child has a reluctance to allow them into their 'space', (often noticeable around the age of 12–18 months, when we expect them to enjoy joint attention), we typically attempt the usual routes: making our voices extremely enthusiastic, physically pulling the child back towards us, talking louder (in case of a hearing problem) and usually resorting to the idea that 'maybe he just wants to be on his own again'. Along the way some things might work, so thankfully we keep them up – rough and tumble, tickling, singing – they all seem to fleetingly bring about a response, but usually there is no method or structure to what we are doing. If you are lucky enough to have an early diagnosis then the deeper understanding as to why your child behaves this way may help – but where do you start?

Communication

How do you create a motivation to communicate?

Observe when your child is most accessible and jot down when these times are. It may be:

- when he's being tickled
- when you sing to him
- when you play rough and tumble
- when he's eating something he really likes
- when he's jumping on the trampoline
- when he's splashing in puddles
- when he's having a bath
- when he's relaxed and in bed.

It may be none of the above but something else, a time when he seems *receptive, relaxed* and willing to look at you (no matter how fleetingly). It may even be a time that you hadn't noticed before, such as sitting in the car (ride as a passenger next to him one day and watch his reactions to you), or swinging in the park.

Once you have pinpointed these times, use them as periods when you really work on showing your child that communication with people *means* something – that it brings its own rewards.

☺   Encourage your child to touch you and create a response that he may find appealing. For example, guide his hand to your face and make a 'beep beep' noise when he touches your nose, or put out your tongue. Make the same response every time so that he realizes that the same gesture creates the same response. He may want to repeat the game over and over.

When he gets the hang of it, make a new gesture for touching different parts of your face. Touch his face and encourage him to make the noise with you. This may be a good game to play last thing at night when he's lying in bed, or when he's in the bath.

☺   When you are engaging in a game he enjoys, such as tickling, stop to take a long pause (often longer than you might feel comfortable with), and wait for your child to make a gesture to indicate he wants the game to continue; this may be by making eye contact or pulling your hands back to him. In response, look back at your child, and say, 'You want more? – yes?' and carry on the game.

☺   *'Peek-a-boo' games* – Hold a cushion/cloth up to your face or hide behind objects (a huge box or play tunnel is great). Create lengthy pauses to build up anticipation and to give your child a space to indicate that he wants the game to continue.

☺   *Pulling silly faces* – Cover your face with your hands and as you take them away change your expression. Try wearing a hat or painting your nose red with lipstick so your child really looks into your face. Encourage eye contact before you change expression.

☺   *Dancing* – Swing and sway to music with your child, then stop and pause for him to indicate he wants more. (See Chapter 6 for lots of dance / music activities.)

☺   Blowing raspberries onto the palms of his hands/tummy – wait for eye contact before you do it again.

Allow your child to dictate how long he lets you into his space – I found that the moment I attempted to prolong an activity and force my attention on my son, then that particular activity ceased to have an appeal to him.

Once you are familiar with how your child responds when he attempts to communicate, look for more and more ways to access him and more opportunities for him to interact.

Ideas to try:

☺   *Balloons* – Simple and often effective, try letting a blown-up balloon deflate and whiz around the room. Let your child anticipate when this will be by saying 'ready, steady – go!' Leave a pause before you let go of the balloon so that your child can anticipate the activity and be motivated to either attempt to say 'go' or make a gesture to communicate it to you such as making eye contact. Novelty shops often sell items powered by balloons, for example, cars that move along the floor or helicopters. These types of shops are not marketed towards very young children but are worth a visit for novelty items that your child would find difficult to ignore. Never leave such things where your child might get hold of them on his own as they may not be safe or have small parts that he may choke on – supervised play only! Try patting a blown-up balloon at your child; if he likes a particular object, draw it onto the surface (or stick a picture of it on the ballon).

☺   *Bubbles* – There's a multitude of different bubble-blowing machines/wands available. Don't forget to wait for your child to make eye contact before you blow more bubbles. If your child wants to blow them too, choose something easy for him to handle (special no-spill containers are also available). If you are initially introducing bubbles to access your child's attention and build motivation to communicate it's best to control the bubble-blowing yourself otherwise the game could soon dissolve into a solitary activity. However, later on, you may wish to use bubbles as a rewarding activity for attempting something more demanding. Encouraging your child to blow is good exercise for those speech muscles or if he's having difficulty blowing himself, try one of the little battery-operated fan/bubble-blowers for instant impact (and easy for him to use too). Also try the bubble wands with built-in fans/whistles. Watch out for the bottle of solution being more interesting than the bubbles! If your child likes containers of this type keep them out of sight and just hand him the wand. Avoid worrying about the carpet by putting towels on the floor so your attention isn't diverted and you can really have fun. (For suppliers of bubble activities, see the back of the book.)

☺   *Feathers* – Some children with autism find the soft touch of a feather very uncomfortable; others (like my son) find it fun to be tickled by it, and to use it to tickle me! Try the really big, brightly coloured plumes you find in sewing and craft shops. Don't just launch at your child with it – play at tickling teddy/siblings/yourself until he starts to take notice and gently try it out on him, leaving long pauses to build up his anticipation.

Remember to make it easy for your child to establish eye contact. Get on your knees at eye level or even underneath your child's eye level. Don't make him have to look up at you.

☺   Share your child's chosen activity. If he runs about the room making noises, copy him! Act as if his behaviour is purposeful and meaningful. After you have imitated him for a while, pause and wait for a reaction. Leave plenty of spaces for him to react if he wants. Try introducing some variations of your own and encourage him to imitate *you.*

☺   If he is holding a toy, act as if he is showing it to you. Hold it up (though don't necessarily take it out of his hands) and talk about it.

☺   *Jack-in-the-box-type toys* – These 'now you see them, now you don't'-type toys are often aimed at babies but have the appeal of instant reward and increase motivation by building anticipation. My son loved the 'frog in a box' toy (by Galt – see references at the back of the book.)

☺   *Attention Grabbers Box* – For sheer practicality, try putting together a box of props you and others can use. I often came across silly novelties that looked like they had potential – some worked, some didn't, but eventually I had a box of little secret weapons. I kept this out of my son's reach. It wasn't an all-purpose toy box. In it was a collection of things which included:

- a spinning top
- a feather
- a glove puppet
- a bubble machine
- a party blower
- a yoyo
- a sticky ball (you threw it against a wall and it slid down slowly!)
- some Sellotape (my son loved the sound)
- a magnetic spinning dolphin.

You might try holding up two items and encouraging your child to point to which he wants – physically mould his hand into a point shape if necessary. Throughout the day encourage this when he goes to grab something, mould his hand into a point and then touch the item before giving him it. Reinforce the gesture by saying, 'Point to…[whatever it is he is requesting].'

NOTE: Always be wary of including something your child likes to the point of obsession otherwise this becomes more important than you or the interaction!

Moving on

When you have found a number of ways to access your child's attention for a few seconds, use these to associate them with another activity, in order to prolong the moment. What you are doing is using something your child finds highly pleasant (for example tickling) and making him associate that with something he probably wouldn't respond to originally – for example, any one of the following:

☺   Singing a commentary.

☺   Saying a commentary to a drum beat.

☺   Using a special hand action rhyme.

☺   Stroking faces and labelling eyes, nose etc…

☺   Playing 'Horsey Horsey' – try a more sedate style than rough and tumble, the focus being on the song.

The case below illustrates how this might be done.

Individual example: Andrew

Three-year-old Andrew loved to be tickled and his parents loved to tickle him. During this time he squealed with delight, he looked into their faces, he allowed them to touch him – he was 'with them'. When the activity stopped, Andrew 'disappeared' again. It was desperately frustrating for his parents to know that he could enjoy sharing space but that this was limited simply to being tickled. They had no idea how to move this on, yet were aware that somehow they needed to develop this pathway.

First they increased the number of times they tickled and rough and tumbled. They had to let go of their idea that this is not how you would interact with a non-autistic child all the time.

Then they began to pair the tickling with another activity – blowing bubbles. Whilst Andrew was being tickled by his mum, his dad would start to blow bubbles. Andrew didn't seem to notice at first but gradually he began to look intently at the bubbles. When he did this his mum would slow down the tickling game to let him focus on the bubbles. During the sessions, Andrew's attention would flit between the two, and he began to touch a specific parent and seek out brief bursts of eye contact with them, depending on which activity he wanted, bubbles or tickles.

The bubbles were then moved to *follow* a bout of tickling (whilst Andrew was still very much with them and enjoying it). Andrew's parents found that he was still receptive to the bubbles and amazed them by reaching out and laughing whilst he tried to pop them. During this time his mum and dad built in long pauses to allow Andrew to communicate that he wanted the game to go on. They were always responsive to whatever gestures and speech attempts he made by saying, 'More bubbles? – yes!' If they felt he was moving into his own solitary space again they would try a tickle, always responding to his lead. If he pulled away they would gradually tail off. If he responded they would keep going. Andrew was always left in control of the duration of the activity.

After a couple of weeks, Andrew responded to the bubbles without having to be tickled as well. Now Andrew's parents had a *second* pathway to access their son; by associating new activities with the old pathways (tickles and bubbles), they continued to have positive results. The next thing they chose was a *singing commentary*. While Dad blew bubbles for Andrew to pop, Mum would begin a singing commentary (to a familiar tune such as 'For he's a jolly good fellow') on what was happening. It went something like this:

> 'Andrew's on the sofa. Andrew's popped a bubble…look, look, a big bubble… Andrew's popped a bubble…Daddy's blowing bubbles…more, more more…Daddy's blowing bubbles…pop, pop, pop…a bubble on the window, a bubble on the floor, look, Andrew bubbles more, more, more…'

Andrew's mum sang the commentary using lots of repetition and rhymes where they were possible, all the time commenting on what Andrew was *actually* doing. It took a couple of sessions before she felt comfortable doing this, but soon found a style that worked and was fun.

Again Andrew originally appeared to ignore the commentary and only focused on the bubbles, but gradually he began to look at his Mum to sing as soon as the bubble game commenced. Once it became clear that the commentary was as important to him as the bubbles, this was then moved on to singing commentaries about other things during the day, for example when Andrew just meandered about the room she would try a commentary on what he was doing;

> 'Looking out of the window, what can you see, I can see a house, I can see a tree, touching the cushion, touching the floor, touching Mummy's knee.'

Over a period of a few weeks, Andrew's parents had created a collection of activities that not only gained Andrew's attention and enabled him to attempt communication, but that were so enjoyable to him that he allowed them to share his space in the same way that only tickling would have done a few weeks previously.

I hope the this example illustrates that even if there is only one activity in which your child seems responsive, there are ways of associating this so closely with a new activity that the same enjoyable feelings allow him to extend the times when he is responsive to your attention and create opportunities for him to communicate.

Most of the parents who completed my survey stated that their children were often more receptive during rough and tumble play, and had worked out by trial and error that there are ways of using these periods to encourage even more interaction; other parents were stuck for ideas on how to move this on. At the time of my son's diagnosis we were aware that he connected with us better and on many levels during this type of play, but were at a loss as to how to use this as a bridge to other activities. Once we eventually discovered how to associate it with new activities, we were able to introduce a range of things that could be used as tools to bring him back to us when he seemed less receptive and as rewards for more demanding activities such as speech therapy.

I would advise that it is counter productive (and totally exhausting!) to attempt to gain your child's attention most of his waking hours. In our early post-diagnosis days, I often panicked if I felt my son had drifted into his own world. I now feel he needs some time to do exactly this. *You* know your child best and can make the decision as to how intensive/relaxed your approach will be and what is right for your child.

As well as these play-based activities to encourage interaction you can also create opportunities for your child to communicate at other times:

☺   Put something your child finds appealing (for example a biscuit) in view but somewhere he cannot reach, or place it inside a sealed transparent container. Wait for your child to make a gesture to you and respond with 'Tom wants…biscuit?

Yes?' and then give him the biscuit. You might try pretending you think he is asking for something else – encourage him to say the name of what he wants.

☺   Create a problem for your child – put his socks on his hands or your wellingtons on his feet. Give him an incentive to communicate that something is wrong.

Once you have discovered there are tools to gain your child's attention and situations that you can create to encourage him to communicate, then some real playing can begin! Always hold on to your secret weapons – you never know when you might need them!

Chapter 3

Structured Play

Why do children on the autism spectrum need structure?

Despite common communication impairments, children on the autism spectrum vary considerably, in fact autism may be seen as an 'umbrella' term in itself, like the description 'learning disability'. As autism does not just affect the ability to learn and understand but affects processing by *all the senses* the potential for its various subtypes is endless – different degrees of problems with speech, social communication, learning difficulties, sensory problems, physical problems...and on top of this are the individual's responses and ability to cope with his condition.

As much as we all hate labels, for most parents the diagnostic label *should* be the passport to relief, to being able to find the most appropriate services, the right professional help and the best approach for them and their child. Confusingly, however, for parents of children on the autism spectrum there doesn't seem to be *one* best approach. There are a number of routes all with worldwide advocates who devoutly believe that this is the only way to help, if not 'recover', your child from autism. For parents of very young children, this diversity of advice is confusing, pressurizing and piles more stress on top of an already strained household.

Despite this barrage of what seems like contradictory advise there are some golden threads of agreement and one such element is that of *structure*. It would appear that those therapies and approaches to autism that have stood the test of time and demonstrated quantifiable results have a central theme of structure. In describing what structure *is*, it is probably easier to describe what structure *isn't*, with all the contradictions that this encompasses!:

- It *isn't* about providing a great deal of *choice* (though creating opportunities for choice is a part of structuring the environment).

- It *isn't* about '*free*' play (though structured play is the first step to encourage spontaneous play).

- It *isn't* about leaving a child to *discover* an activity, its limits and potentials by himself (though learning to discover these things together is a definite goal).

It isn't about these things because in a play context, choice, freedom and discovery are simply *not* the things that motivate children with autism to play the way their non-autistic peers do. Children with autism need structure because despite their many differences, in general they have impaired motivation to interact, learn and play. They have rigid and repetitive patterns of thinking and therefore of talking and playing, and are often motivated to preserve 'sameness'. Coupled with a resistance to being directed and a need to take control of as many aspects of their immediate environment as possible, it is not difficult to appreciate how being part of a learning and playing environment that advocates spontaneity, free choice and independent discovery simply is not appropriate for a child with autism.

What does structuring play actually mean and how does it work?

You might feel this sounds fine in a therapeutic or educational environment, but how does this work in a busy home environment with a three-year-old? We shouldn't feel that the *only* way to help our child is to follow a specific private programme executed by a therapist, not a mere mortal parent! As primary carers for our children we can learn how to structure their play – it's about choosing an activity, looking at how your child already engages (or doesn't) in the activity, whether he plays appropriately or inappropriately, how he interacts with you during these times (or doesn't) and how you can make improvements. It's about looking at his day and working out how you can steer him into constructive interaction and play for more hours than he currently does. Introducing structure is also about being aware of what makes him distressed and working out how communication can be improved to make him feel safer by making his day seem more predictable and less chaotic. It's also about taking some control yourself; making your child aware that he is a part of a functioning family, with the comings and goings that this involves, and not always the nucleus that the rest of the family revolves around. Giving your child structure allows you to do this in the kindest way.

Structuring play works by systematically breaking a play activity into its component parts so that it is no longer a jumble of language, objects and actions that has no meaning for your child. By breaking it down into very simple elements you give your child a chance to work out what each element represents – you give him the chance to interpret the activity and give it meaning. Fundamentally you are giving his brain a chance to keep up with processing incoming information. I expect achievements will vary according to your child's potential but even the smallest of successes will justify the effort. This is how structuring an *individual* activity works. Throughout the book I also refer to structuring the day as a series of activities. These will not all be play activities – the day is represented in pictures showing the sequence in which they will happen, including the particular play activities that you have planned for that day.

Creating play opportunity – setting the stage

Each of the following chapters in turn draws your attention to sensory problems that may hinder playing with that particular activity and the importance of checking the play environment, so I won't repeat this again here.

Remember to be responsive to your child's level of tolerance to direct requests – if he is resistant, pull back; introduce the activity that you have planned into the day 'indirectly'. Play alongside your child as if for your own pleasure, set up a duplicate activity within his reach and keep the session very short (one or two minutes at a time). If you feel that introducing structured play and learning is 'beyond' your child at the moment, concentrate on the less invasive forms of interaction, such as the activities described in Chapters 6 and 8, as well as the ideas on 'sharing space' detailed in Chapter 2.

When you begin to systematically 'teach' a child with autism to play, it helps if you have worked out a few things beforehand:

- *Exactly* which objects you will be using – 'exactly' means just that, have ready only the toys/materials that you will need for that particular activity. Decide if things such as the box they come in will be distracting and, if so, remove them.

- Know what the play area will be – the living room floor/a table/a tray top/a rug. Does your child need a prop to remind him that this is where his focus of attention will be, a special cushion to sit on, or a picture card reminding him to stay seated?

- If you are using picture prompts (the importance of visual supports is explained at the end of the chapter), check they are not confusing or ambiguous or that your child is not interpreting them too literally. If you experience problems with the pictures supplied at the back of the book, adapt them to your child – photocopy them, then white-out with correction fluid and redraw elements where necessary.

- Are you going to use a reward or reinforcer for your child after he has completed an activity – something tangible to motivate him to attempt it? Do you have a card to communicate this to your child? For further details on re-inforcers see Chapter 4.

- How long do you expect your child to engage in the activity? How simple or complicated are your goals? What actions and or interactions do you specifically want your child to achieve? This may be something as simple as turn-taking with stacking rings or as complicated as an imaginary play sequence with a set of figures.

When you have answered these questions and have the materials and objects to hand, you have set the stage.

Breaking play down into tasks

Once again this sounds like a technical term for a common-sense approach to working with any child with a learning disability. Even for children without additional learning difficulties, their autism impairs the ability to generalise and learn. To break down a play activity we have to look at it as a series of tasks and teach each task separately. This may sound like taking play and removing all the fun – the hard part is not breaking the activity into its separate tasks, it's keeping it fresh and lively and motivating. If your child picks up on your voice being desperate for him to comply or worse still annoyed at his non-compliance, he's likely to resist.

The following example illustrates these points.

Playing the magnetic fishing game

The goal – to play 'turn taking' with a magnetic fishing game.

The materials – magnetic fishing games, which are available in many toy shops. Do remember to get an easy-to-handle one or alternatively make a simple version yourself by doing the following:

Cut a piece of fabric or card into a pond shape. Make six cardboard fish with paper clips attached to their mouths. Make a rod from a piece of dowel and string, and attach a strong magnet to the end of the string.

The tasks –

- To lift the rod up slowly with the fish on, after the parent has steered the magnet to the fish.
- To attach the magnet himself with his hands and then lift the rod clear.
- To attach the magnet by dangling it over the fish.
- To 'turn take' with two fish.
- To 'turn take' with six fish.
- To add picture cards for him to label on the reverse side of the fish, or to put numbers on the reverse side. Whoever has the highest number, wins.

Even though this is highly structured in some ways, there are no set rules. Some children might get the hang of an activity very quickly and skip straight through all the tasks; others might need extra help from you in motivating them to look at the activity and attempt the first task. Accomplishing each task can be seen as a separate play session – a general 'fishing game' picture prompt can be used for each session. The first example session might go as follows:

> The materials are set up. Mum and Adam collect the fishing game picture card off his diary board (see later section, 'Structuring the Day'). The next picture card is of Adam's reward/reinforcer – listening to music.

Mum: Now it's time to play 'fishing'. Let's get the card, Adam.

> (Adam ignores her and picks up the music card.)

Mum: Yes Adam…after the fishing game we'll play music.

> (Adam still resists a little.)

Mum: I can see…a yellow fish and a rod!

> (Mum takes the fish and makes it pretend to swim. She then picks it up and drops it, saying 'it's got away…come back naughty fish!'…she plays as if for her own pleasure.)

> (Adam stands on the fish.)

Mum: Well done, you caught it…it's got your toes!

> (Mum makes the fish tickle Adam's toes.)

> (Adam sits down.)

> (Mum puts the rod in his hands and closes her hand around his. They lift the fish out together with a 'One two three…wheee!' Mum puts the magnet on the fish and lays the rod on the floor. Adam stands up and starts to walk away.)

> Mum: It's ready to go 'One two three Wheee!' Adam – (Mum points to the rod) Adam do 'One two three wheee', then listen to music.
>
> (Mum physically guides his hand to the rod.)
>
> (Adam finally crouches and lifts the rod – Mum touches his elbow, saying 's..l..o..w..l..y')
>
> Mum: Yes well done – Adam did it, let's listen to music.

The next two or three play sessions could be spent trying to make simply lifting the fish up fun and motivating so that completing the play activity is not simply a means to reaching the reward. Be as silly and creative as you can be:

- Vary the 'fish' – draw colours or stick pictures on them.

- Stick a chocolate button or Smartie eye on the fish with masking tape folded over on itself to make it double sided, (you might try Sellotape but make it less sticky by pressing it onto your clothes a few times first).

- Make the fish 'do' things that may make your child laugh.

This is where parents and carers really have to work hard. Non-autistic children simply don't need to be taught step-by-step that this is a fun activity – understanding the meaning of the game and what it represents just happens, and any additional fun is just that…an extra bonus. Children with autism will struggle to understand: 'Why do I need to do this thing?' Your job is to teach your child that playing, and interaction, are fun!

On the basis of this example, any activity (not necessarily just play) can be broken down into a number of tasks that can be taught separately. In the same way that '*back chaining*' can be used to complete jigsaws (your child places in the last piece, then the last two pieces etc.), it can also be used for any play task. Your child's first play session is completing the last task *after* you have guided him through the rest, i.e. he lifts the rod after you have attached it to the fish and put the rod in his hand. After he understands and can do each stage, take him back one more step, i.e. next stage he attaches the fish to the magnet, then next stage he dangles the rod over the fish to catch it, etc.

Analyzing play activities in this way takes some practice but very quickly becomes simply your way of playing with your own child. You may already have been doing this to an extent without even realizing exactly what you were doing!

Applied behavioural analysis (ABA)

Many readers have probably heard of Lovaas or ABA training. This is one of the long-standing therapies that have a central theme of structure which has proved positive for many children. Two years ago we ourselves considered the programme but decided that for us and our little boy this was not going to be the right decision. We were, however, in a good position to offer a high level of structure and one-to-one attention ourselves, and felt strongly that we also had to create a learning and playing environment that accommodated his autism to some extent. The choice to go down this route is highly individual but any parent who hasn't heard of the therapy should at least research it. In brief, the home-based programme consists of teaching sessions conducted by a team of helpers trained by an ABA supervisor. The therapy can be intensive – up to 40 hours a week – and costly (though there are ways of trying to get help with this). Children are taught skills in a similar way to some of the techniques that I describe in this book – breaking them down into smaller tasks and using reinforcers to motivate. Many programmes are 'play'-orientated and have come a long way since the older style 'behaviour'-orientated programmes which have received negative publicity in the past.

ABA is a big commitment emotionally, physically and financially, but for *some* families it is the preferred route. Those with children on the programme are usually more than willing to let you see how it works and to share their experiences. Like all therapeutic routes, parents need to explore all the possible ramifications and make an informed decision whilst trying not to get bogged down by the latest 'recovery' programme. This book is about demonstrating that as parents we have the power to help ourselves to knowledge and information in order to help our children.

For more information on ABA and other therapeutic options see the resources at the back of the book.

Structuring early learning

Non-autistic children have a curiosity and motivation to understand as much of the world around them as possible. Their developing brains cope with new concepts and levels of understanding as soon as they are physically ready. Their ability to think and reason is aided by a stimulating and attentive environment as well as their own biological make-up.

If however, that very biological make-up is impaired in a way that takes away the motivation to understand and make sense of the child's surrounding world (the way an autism spectrum disorder does) then the process of learning is disabled, regardless of whether the child's intellectual reasoning is intact.

This makes the prospect of creating an environment to support learning much more of a challenge. Most parents of children with autism are in agreement that their child needs to have proactive input into helping him *learn* and *play* and *communicate* as early as possible. Even though these three elements of development are very much entwined, we might see them also as separate arenas that need equal attention. From the outside, activities aimed at developing play skills may also look like activities to aid learning and communication and vice-versa. For parents, however, it may help to allocate structured time to the three different activities, even though the activities eventually support each other. Activities specifically designed to aid communication (speech and language therapy) should be provided at your child's individual level of ability. Make the most of your speech and language therapist for this. *Structured learning* can be done as a daily session at home, taking the form of a slightly more formal version of the structured play activities. Try creating a 'workbox' that is brought out every day, preferably at the same time of day. Keep it out of your child's reach and rotate and change the materials often to keep his interest. To start with, keep the session very short with two or three two-minute activities, and gradually try to build up the time to a longer session. Use activities that can be done at a table top – you might like to sit opposite your child so that he can see your face, but if this is too intrusive for him at first, sit at his side.

For ideas of what items to put in your workbox and how to introduce them, see Chapter 5 ('Table-Top Games and Puzzles'). Mix these with exercises provided by your speech and language therapist, and some pen control exercises (see Chapter 12, 'Being Creative – Art and Craft').

Individual example: Sam

> Sam was three years old and recently diagnosed with an autism spectrum disorder. Since the diagnosis, Sam's parents had been working on increasing his eye contact and generally gaining his attention with some simple play activities. Sam had very few words that he used consistently, but his parents felt he was actually quite bright and able but his hyperactivity and rigid routines were preventing him from learning. They had started to help him communicate with a

picture diary and had created a box containing a variety of learning activities that was to be brought out after breakfast (a time when Sam seemed to be at his best) every day. They took a photo of the box and gave it the label 'workbox'. They also had a picture card for television, which they were using as a reward (Sam liked to watch a particular video over and over). At first Sam resisted having to sit, but when he realized the first session was for only one minute he became compliant enough to sit for ten minutes by the end of the first week.

In the box were:

- a shape-matching puzzle
- four photos of familiar people and animals (his brother Tom, Daddy, Grandma, Fluffy) – Sam was asked to 'give Mummy Fluffy' etc.
- a furry toy dog and a brush – Sam was asked to brush dog's nose, ears, feet, tail etc.

After he had completed each activity, Sam put the item(s) back in the box. After the final one he was 'rewarded' with his video. Sam always resisted spontaneously being directed in this way outside the workbox session, but actually looked forward to the sessions (and their rewards!) when he knew it was going to happen. For two years, until Sam started school, he continued the daily sessions. By the time he was five he was completing two twenty-minute sessions a day in which he was recognizing written words, making story sequences with sequencing picture cards, categorising objects and building on reasoning skills. During this period they went through times when he occasionally refused to comply; if this happened then the reward was changed and the activities rethought, or sometimes Sam just needed a couple of days off!

These structured learning sessions are not the only times for learning. Modelling correct behaviour and language and creating opportunities to communicate should be done throughout the day, but often it is difficult for a child with autism to spontaneously attend to what you are saying in order to listen and learn. At the table you have a few minutes when you really 'have him', and the structure and predictability of this connection feels less stressful for him than being randomly invaded. Always be responsive when your child initiates an interaction (verbal or otherwise) at other times during the day.

Structuring the day – creating a visual diary

Throughout the book I make reference to using 'picture prompts' to communicate to your child which play activity you have planned. There are some for you to photocopy and use at the back of this book. Using picture prompts in this way is an idea from TEACCH (Treatment and Education of Autistic and Communication Handicapped Children) – for more information, see the references at the back of the book. It makes sense to use these prompt cards as part of a picture diary to communicate the course of the day's events to your child. How you display and use the cards is a personal choice – you may display them left to right, horizontally or in a vertical strip, top to bottom. Make them durable enough to withstand a fair amount of use; either invest in a laminator, or stick them to card and cover them with sticky-backed plastic. You could use a piece of 'hook and loop' so that they can be peeled off and reused.

How many cards you use is up to you and your child. Some children may need prompts for getting dressed and using the toilet; others may only need them for outings and activities. You might find the prompts relieve a long-standing problem caused by the frustrations of poor communication. For a number of months we had a problem if we went out and our son didn't know which car (Mummy's or Daddy's) or which parent he was going with. After I had made cards for all the permutations – both parents in Dad's car, both in Mum's car, Dad in Mum's car etc – the problem suddenly lifted. I used simple stick 'men' and 'women' drawings (plus a stick child) and luckily the cars are different colours! Picture representations can be made for anything, including a sequenced set of cards to depict the order in which to dress, wash hands etc.

The website *www.dotolearn.com* has a great selection of copyright pictures that you can simply print off and use.

A morning in pictures might look something like this:

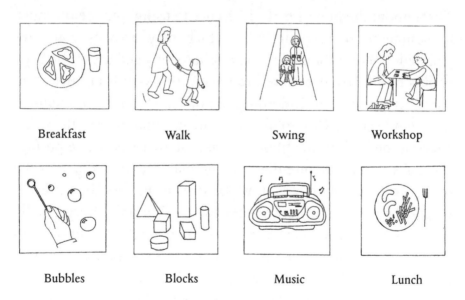

| Breakfast | Walk | Swing | Workshop |

| Bubbles | Blocks | Music | Lunch |

After an activity is complete, have a posting box or envelope for your child to put the picture card in to indicate that is the end, then return to the board for the next activity.

Introducing choice and flexibility

Even though choice and flexibility are difficult areas for children with autism, after your child is used to using picture prompts you can also use them to help him make choices. His first choice may be which reward to have, for example 'biscuit' or 'video'. You might also use them to help him choose an activity for 'free play', for example 'trampoline' or 'cars'. Don't put all the choices on the board; provide two, from which he can choose one and give it to you. Physically giving the card to you and gaining a response demonstrates to him that communication not only involves others, but that it works.

- Using pictures to aid communication appeals to the 'visual learner' – children with autism usually think and learn visually.

- Pictures help to prepare him mentally for the next task and allow him to 'shift gear', reducing anxiety and confusion.

- Pictures are excellent communication aids; their motivating and 'attention-grabbing' qualities make them suitable not only for non-verbal children but for all children on the autism spectrum.

- Pictures are a physical aid to help your child exercise choice and control.

Once you've started using picture prompts, give your child plenty of time to associate the picture with the activity. It's tempting to give up too soon if this takes some time. However, if you stick with it you should gain a tool that will reclaim some order in all of your lives.

Chapter 4

Toys, Toys, Toys

Help – my child won't play with his toys!

A non-autistic child's initial and most interesting playthings are his parents. From day one, a baby seeks out faces and human voices as if pre-programmed to 'relate'. After only a few weeks he will have a two-way 'conversation' with Mum, making a gesture, copying and waiting for a reaction rather like a conversation without words. He does this because it is fun, it makes him feel good; he is playing! If we see this early impulse to interact as a springboard to later language and play skills, in children with autism, where motivation and ability to relate are impaired, it would be fair to say that right from the start they have missed out on developing a primary skill.

By the time their child is 18 months old, one of the first 'autistic' signs that worries parents is a lack of motivation to play, or an obsession with a particular type of activity, such as lining up cars rather than playing with them. We can make excuses for slow language development at this age but although it is often difficult to pinpoint, there is a pattern to the child's general lack of interest in people and toys that parents find disconcerting.

In non-autistic children, playing with a simple toy such as a rattle is often part of an interaction: the baby shakes the rattle,

Mum looks into the baby's face and makes a pleasing sound. As the child gets older, he allows direction and encouragement from Mum – often (non-verbally) seeking her advice for where to put something, for example, holding up a brick to her or part of a puzzle. *Jointly* they attend to whatever the activity is, and all the time the child is learning to imitate by watching and inquiring.

For children with autism, direction and attention from other people is often uncomfortable and unpleasant, causing overload and such a sense of invasion that the child shuts off, diverts his attention or retaliates. The acclaimed writer Donna Williams (who has autism herself), calls this response 'exposure anxiety' (try reading *Exposure Anxiety: The Invisible Cage* – see 'Recommended Reading' for details). It is for this reason that direction and 'head-on' interaction with your child can be met with such a negative reaction and directed play and learning should be kept to small manageable bursts.

In summary, joint play with toys is difficult for children with autism due to:

- problems with imitation, interaction and joint attention

- problems with generalisation of skills, for example, difficulty applying an idea or skill learnt for one activity to a different context

- difficulty accepting direction from an adult and the resulting 'exposure anxiety' that this can cause

- problems with flexibility, for example, having a set way of playing with an item, such as only building towers with bricks

- problems with imagination – not being able to imagine a situation other than here and now or being another identity, such as problems with dressing up, pretending games

- problems with meaning – difficulty imagining that items can represent other things, for example, a saucepan could be a banjo, or a helmet or a drum.

- communication difficulties, both in expressing and understanding language

- problems with sensory processing – being bombarded by a variety of sensory input and not being able to filter it out in order to focus on the activity at hand.

Reassessing existing toys: back to basics

Right up to the time a child is either diagnosed autistic or the parent has a strong suspicion that that this might be the case, parents and carers have usually tried to introduce toys to the child in the usual way they would with a regular toddler. After a year or so, the rattles and soft bricks go and in come the shape sorters and stacking rings. After another year, out these go and in come the tea sets and fire engines! Somewhere along the line is the awful realization that very few of these things have been played with/responded to, or if they were touched it was in odd and unusual ways. My son's favorite object at the age of two was a teapot, which he repeatedly filled with tiny bricks and he would scream hysterically when he could not fit in any more. In fact, any toy which could be used as a container was played with, in a fashion, but this wasn't a satisfactory way of playing, even for him. Eventually there were always tears and frustrations. Other parents have reported that their children simply ignored or hid their toys or, in one case, the mother of an older verbal child replied in the survey that he simply asked for them to be 'put away in the attic'.

Although there are a variety of structured therapies/ programmes that parents can use with their children, they generally have the same attitude to toys – *less is best* at any one time, for a variety of reasons:

- Most children have problems to differing degrees with decoding information. Donna Williams wrote in her book *Autism: An Inside–Out Approach*, p.92:

  'For much of my childhoood … things that were meant to be tuned out weren't, these things were all competing for processing when they shouldn't have been. I was jumping between processing the white of the page as well as the print, the flicker of the light and shadow as well as the objects themselves, the sounds of the people moving about in between syllables of words being said at the time, the rustle of clothing and the sound of my own voice.'

Given that this is the case it makes sense to keep the amount of information to which you expose your child to a minimum, at least until you yourself are aware of when he appears to have reached his threshold. This means introducing toys one at a time so that you can help him see an item; for example a toy car as a *whole* rather than a collection of *parts*, at the same time minimizing background noise and scaling down your own speech.

- A 'collection' of articles has the potential to be played with inappropriately and obsessively, for example stacked in cupboards or on top of each other/thrown /balanced.

- Your child might see a particular toy that he isn't playing with which triggers a rapid stream of associations that will interfere with his concentration on the immediate task. For example, whilst playing with the object you have selected he might see out of the corner of his eye a soft toy and make the following connections: Winnie the Pooh – video tape – juice (because he always has juice whilst watching this tape). He might then suddenly be frantically requesting juice pulling you into the kitchen whilst you have to guess what he is requesting.

Being organized

Actively working at helping your child to play means preparing activities the night before and introducing new activities carefully and mindfully of any problems that might occur. This doesn't mean that your playing should be sterile and unspontaneous – anticipating when your child is open and accessible means precisely the opposite – improvising and being spontaneous to squeeze out the potential of every learning situation. However, it does mean having a plan , short-term and long-term goals. Don't be a martyr spending hours every evening – you'll be exhausted and resentful, but thirty minutes will save you the stress of trying to rush around pulling toys out, putting others away, thinking about what to do and at the same time keeping your child safe and happy!

Picture prompts for playing

For every play activity, try to have a picture card – there are some at the end of the book that can be enlarged or photocopied, you can also use photographs, catalogue pictures of toys or try making your own simple line drawing (see Chapter 13 for 'stick figure' illustrations). Also have a card to represent whatever reward/ re-inforcer will happen after the activity (these are discussed later in the chapter).

The previous chapter (Chapter 3, 'Structured Play') details how to use the picture cards as part of a visual diary for the day's events. Remember to allow your child to associate the picture with the activity initially by positioning it so that it is visible whilst you are doing that activity.

If your child does not use spoken language at all you may want to use PECS (Picture Exchange Communication System). PECS is an alternative and augmentative communication system for children and adults with communication difficulties. The PECS system should always be implemented by a trained practitioner – your speech and language therapist should be able to help. For more information, see the references at the back of the book.

Getting started: ideas

☺   As well as your 'attention grabbers' box, which is kept out of reach but within easy access for yourself (see Chapter 2), also have a collection of five–six large boxes (lidded plastic storage boxes are ideal), which can be rotated every day.

The reasons for having several boxes rather than one big one are that children with autism tend to:

- have poor attention spans and may well flit between toys without directing attention to any one in particular

- not know which toys they have unless they are items of obsession

- have language difficulties that make requesting a particular toy frustrating

- have imagination problems, which means that varying toys every day keeps up interest. A non-autistic child might play every day with his farm set making elaborate stories in his head and learning new skills with the same toy. A child with autism who has some playing skills is still only likely to manage two–five minute sessions with any one particular item.

Varying toys builds in flexibility and prevents your child becoming fixated on having one collection of items which he expects and needs to see in the same place every day (yet is still unlikely to play with).

☺   Try creating a theme with each box, e.g. houses, animals. Here are some examples of what to put in the boxes:

Theme: houses

- A book with a theme (e.g. houses).
- A jigsaw featuring a house/kitchen or furniture.
- Play dough (cutter shape that might make a house).
- A picture of a house to colour in.
- Two teddies/dolls/teacups, teapot, wash cloth, toothbrush.
- Bricks (enough to make two simple houses – one for you, one for your child).
- Dolls' furniture (changing the furniture weekly for example kitchen, then bathroom etc…). Be careful using a dolls house if your child is drawn to 'container' style activities, for example filling cupboards etc. A dolls' house might just become another cupboard to stack things in! Try playing on a table opposite each other with these items first; if you want to introduce a house and a problem arises – simple, remove the doors!

Theme: animals

- Plastic farm animals – see Chapter 13 for how to create a play sequence.
- 'Make a scene' (sticker scene book) – farmyard.

- Noise makers (the tubs which produce an animal sound when they are turned over). Your child makes the sound and you help him match the sound to the appropriate animal.

- Animal snap (see Chapter 7 for turn-taking games).

- Sticking an animal picture (see Chapter 12 for ideas).

- Matching plastic animals to their pictures (see Chapter 5).

- An animal jigsaw.

Other ideas for themes

- Shapes

- Shopping

- Cooking/food

- Feelings

- People

- Weather

- Doctors

- Gardens

- Family

☺ Character Theme Boxes

Some children have a specific interest in a favourite TV character, such as Thomas the Tank Engine and probably have a collection of related jigsaws etc. By having these in one box you can move between different activities yet still use a familiar, comforting image. Include play dough and paper etc. so you can make items related to the theme (for example play dough toast for 'Teletubbies', or a drawing of Postman Pat's cat). Keeping all these items together means that you don't run the risk of putting a Noddy book, for example, in another box, making your child reluctant to play with anything other than Noddy for that day! You can also use the associated video as a reward at the end of the play sessions.

After approximately two to three weeks, change the items in the boxes around; add new activities and put others in storage for a few weeks.

Use the chapters throughout the book for ideas on *how* to play with the individual items in your play boxes, such as:

- Indirect parallel play with a duplicate item – sit alongside your child with the same toy that he has – this may be a musical instrument, a toy car, some bricks etc. Copy what he does no matter how random (or inappropriate), put the object in your mouth, copy his noises. Scan your child constantly to see if he is watching you. Use some of his actions and change them – see if he will imitate your actions. Give a gentle, simple commentary and stop for pauses – watch your child, see if he will stop, respond to any gestures he makes as an attempt to communicate that he wants to carry on.

- Short burst of directed play – broken into its separate tasks (see Chapter 3).

- A structured play sequence using a picture script (see Chapter 13).

Use the approach that is right for your child and his level of communication and readiness to interact. Aim to spend five minutes or more on each activity with good breaks in between. Sometimes you might not manage two minutes, other days your child may surprise you and engage for an half an hour. As always, follow his lead.

Individual example: Sally

Sally had a toy cooker from the age of two. She was now three and a half and had only ever used it like a cupboard – packing clothes, books and dolls into it and throwing the toy pans and food around the room.

Sally's Mum had created a series of play boxes and was working on increasing the times Sally was engaged with her throughout the day. Sally loved potato crisps and her Mum was using these (sparingly) as 'reinforcers' during these play sessions. Sometimes she also used Sally's favourite activity of drawing a series of long straight lines on paper as a reward.

Sally's Mum decided to remove the toy cooker altogether and created a new play box, themed on food. She put in it:

- two dolls, plates and plastic food – for pretend feeding
- two plastic pans, two spoons and two pieces of card with gas rings drawn on them – for pretend cooking
- play dough to make pretend food
- a reusable sticker book featuring food
- a book about 'helping Mummy cook'.

Using a picture prompt for 'doll play' and a picture prompt for crisps, Sally's Mum introduced the doll play by having a doll, plate and play food of her own and setting one up for Sally. She commenced playing as if purely for her own pleasure and kept the game up for quite a while on her own. When Sally eventually copied her Mum feeding dolly, her Mum praised her by saying 'Good – Sally fed dolly' (so Sally knew exactly what it was her Mum was pleased with). Her

Mum then gave her a crisp and introduced it into the play as 'a crisp for dolly, a crisp for Sally' – a turn-taking game that made Sally laugh. After a few sessions playing this way they moved on to pretend cooking on the cardboard gas rings, making food from play dough and reading about cooking with Mummy.

After a few weeks the cooker was reintroduced. Mum still did the activity alongside Sally and made sure there were no other toys/articles around to put inside the cooker. Sally was now using the toy appropriately, the gas rings looked like those they had played with before drawn on cardboard, the pans were the same ones she was used to and her play had meaning and purpose (to feed dolly). Sally still needed Mum to structure the sessions and when the activity was over, the cooker was put away. After another couple of weeks they added pretend shopping and helping with some real cooking.

Sources of toys

Use the toys you already have but be aware of what you might need when on shopping trips (rather than buying on impulse and regretting later). A good source of items are car boot sales, charity shops, toy fairs as well as the shops and mail order companies listed at the back of the book. It is always wise to buy toys on your own or at least out of sight and introduce them appropriately in your structured play sessions rather than allowing initial free play in which your child might create a rigid play pattern which he will not deviate from. Remember, if something seems beyond your child's abilities now but is a good bargain, buy it and store it for later.

What to look for in appropriate toys

- Items should not frustrate by demanding the use of fine motor skills (manipulation using hands/fingers) in advance of your child's ability. Keep toy figures, tea sets etc. a good size that your child can handle easily. If the activity is designed precisely to work fine motor skills, such as threading or lacing, use big beads with a large hole and stiff cord (try wrapping sticky tape around the end of the cord to make it easier to push through the hole). This way your child builds confidence without frustration and can complete the task quickly without losing attention.

- Toys that have parts that fit inside each other or interlock should do so easily. If you have to match up fiddly parts yourself then your child might have great difficulty and get very distressed or simply lose interest.

- Children with autism tend to relate to realistic items that don't require leaps of imagination – i.e. toy telephones that look like real ones rather than brightly patterned ones with lots of features.

- Toys should be visually unfussy – for example plain tea sets rather than those covered in busy patterns.

- Find toys which do not have parts that are likely to fall off, for example vulnerable pieces which stick out and might snap off.

- Jigsaws should be simple, chunky and lie flat. Insert jigsaw boards have a satisfying and definite fit.

Remember when choosing toys not to judge their suitability by the age level indicated on the box. Look at it carefully and imagine your child playing with it first.

Separating toys into challengers and reinforcers

All the toys in the play boxes can be seen as 'challengers'; i.e. they would probably *not* be spontaneously picked up and played with appropriately. They will *challenge* your child's play skills and there will be a limited amount of time in which he is willing and able to play with them. To motivate him to play with these toys you need a reinforcer or reward (something that reinforces that the play activity was actually enjoyable because something happened during or at the end of the activity which was pleasant). If your child has obsessive items/routines you cannot simply remove these; they'll quickly be replaced with another routine, causing much distress in the mean time. Instead, use these items and activities separately, away from the play boxes, as rewards for joint play sessions.

In summary, reinforcers are the toys, objects, activities your child would *voluntarily* choose to engage in or find attractive to watch. They differ from child to child and are often not what we might think of as playing. They might be:

- spinning lids, tops, wheels
- simply carrying an object from room to room
- a collection of items that are arranged in a specific way or items that form part of an elaborate routine
- attractive things to look at or that make pleasing noises to your child – glitter tubes, bubble tubes, party blowers, whistles etc.
- ripping paper
- edible rewards – raisins, crisps, or even chocolate (though make teeth-cleaning part of the routine).

It is likely that these types of activity are what would fill most of your child's time if he were allowed. In addition, there are the activities (or 'stims') that require no objects – bodily spinning, hand flapping, pacing, rocking, vocal noises, opening and shutting doors.

Initially these might become the reinforcers; the rewards your child can have after an attempted play activity and can be given an encompassing verbal or picture label such as 'break time' (see picture prompts at the back of the book).

Allowing self-stimulatory and seemingly autistic behaviour as rewards might seem like you're not making progress, but bear in mind that you will be:

- reducing the number of hours a day that your child engages in this type of activity
- using the behaviours positively as a way to coax your child into interactions with you
- allowing your child the comfort and relaxation to be who he is.

There are some autistic behaviours such as self-harming (head banging, biting etc.) that obviously cannot be allowed in this way. Ways of reducing these behaviours need to be addressed in conjunction with your clinical psychologist – ask for help.

Eventually your aim is to introduce more *appropriate* reward activities that include interaction: bubbles, singing, rough-and-tumble tickling games, balloon games etc. (see Chapter 2 for further ideas).

Communication and interaction as rewards in themselves are the ultimate reinforcer but until your child can get beyond his autistic drive to avoid social interaction and enjoy the benefits that it brings, his motivation to attempt such activities must come from something more tangible to him.

Your child, however, will always need some time simply to be who he is and that includes expressing his autism. To aim to eradicate all traces of his autistic behavior would be highly stressful for both you and him and would have negative consequences all round.

Modifying existing toys to remove stress

Any toy your child might fixate on during your play sessions should be left out of the play boxes and, where possible, adapted. My own son would soon forget that the toy iron was for pretend ironing and would get absorbed in balancing the flex in impossible configurations. By removing strings and toy flexes from such items, initially they became less attractive but then we could start to learn to play with them all over again, appropriately. It's best to remove such things before your child sees it in the first place. However, if this is not possible, take the toy out of circulation for a few weeks and reintroduce it later. If the obsessional part is integral to the toy itself, for example, spinning wheels on cars, then leave this type of toy out of the play boxes all together and use this activity as a reward instead (though make sure you play in parallel with a similar toy).

The importance of realism

Realism is a recurring theme throughout this book and is an important concept to be aware of during your 'playing' times. The communication and imagination deficiencies your child has mean that much of his knowledge of the world is based on what he sees and participates in. Learning to *imitate* is a fundamental play skill. At first, it will be easier for your child to imitate simple everyday actions which have *real* meaning to him than for him to imitate complex imaginative sequences. Throughout the day there are many real-life imitation opportunities, for example:

- washing pots
- unloading/loading washing machine
- cooking
- using tools
- shopping
- sweeping.

If your child would rather use your actual equipment than his toy versions, try to accommodate this where it can be done safely, for example, for chopping real food such as mushrooms, give him a blunt knife. For washing up, provide a set of safety steps to reach the sink and for sweeping, use a real dustpan and brush. If he shows interest and motivation to attempt these sort of activities, go with it. It may be tempting to deflect an activity because it may be messy or is not one of your structured sessions for the day, but any motivation to imitate should be nurtured.

It may be that your child is having difficulty relating to a toy because he needs a realistic context. For example, he may need a road for his cars to go on, with a starting point and an end point – try drawing a road on a piece of card. Place a house and a garage (if you use one) at one end and at the other end place a petrol station or park (or anything else your child is familiar with visiting in the car). Keep it very simple to start with – show him the car leaving the house to visit the park and then coming back to the house. Try to keep items in proportion so they 'look right', and create contexts for doll and teddy play using baths, beds and tables. Make fields for farm animals from cardboard or green felt, and cages for zoo animals from boxes. Put plastic sea creatures in tanks of water. Look at his play and use props to fill in what his imagination needs.

Specific useful toys

A basic set of useful items to help with your play would include the following:

☺   A chunky shape sorter – today there are shape sorters and stacking rings that reward a correct response with a noise or flashing lights (see the back of the book for suppliers).

☺   A collection of easy-to-handle human figures and dolls' furniture.

☺   A simple collection of farm animals.

☺   'Make a scene cards' with reusable stickers.

☺   Simple two-, three-, four-piece jigsaws (any number your child can handle easily).

☺   Jigsaw boards where pieces slot into pre-cut shapes.

☺   Toy food/tea set/shopping basket.

☺   Threading games.

☺   Soft easy-to-catch ball.

☺   A number of bean bags. (For ideas on more physical play toys see Chapter 8.)

☺   Blocks – rather than bricks. Blocks allow greater flexibility and avoid the possibility of your child getting stuck on building long towers every time. Wooden building blocks can be used in a variety of ways:

• Matching games – match bricks to pictures of their shape or colour.

- 'Ready, steady, go' games – building and knocking down towers teaches your child to wait for your cue.

- Make simple two-/three-piece models for your child to copy.

☺   *Magnetic blocks* – sets of magnetic blocks can be purchased from specialist educational suppliers. They can combine in various ways to make a number of specific articles and cannot be used like bricks to simply build long towers. They fit together well and do not have the frustrating habit of breaking apart.

☺   Toys which can be used as part of a 'ready, steady, go' sequence, for example, a ball/marble run, domino men (see the back of the book for suppliers) or even a bubble tube that can be turned over to send bubbles floating back up to the top. These types of activities have an element of anticipation and reward, and they encourage attention as well as creating opportunities for your child to attempt to communicate that he wants the activity again by either saying 'more', or showing you an intentional gesture to mean 'again', such as a nod or reaching out to the toy.

Birthdays and Christmas

Children with autism often find the bombardment of 'newness' on special occasions stressful and unpleasant. The social contact involved when giving and receiving presents can also be difficult. To tackle these problems you might like to try the following:

- Only give one present at a time and give your child plenty of time to look at it and work out what it is. Any other presents can be filtered in over a few days.

- If wrapped presents cause your child concern as to what's inside, try wrapping them in cellophane (this way he still gets to 'unwrap' his gift yet can see what it is), or draw the item on the gift tag, or put a catalogue picture on the gift tag.

- Don't force your child to open presents from other people in front of them if he doesn't want to. Model good manners by saying slowly and deliberately, 'That's really kind of you – thank you, we'll open it later' (friends and family will not be offended). This way you can find out what's inside and prepare your child. Children with autism find it hard to be polite and hide disappointment, which can make receiving gifts awkward. Often a present might be very useful (like a book) but not immediately attractive to your child. If this is the case, don't make an issue of unwrapping the present; gently filter the book into your reading sessions (see Chapter 14).

- On the run up to Christmas and birthdays make a list of items that would be suitable and appropriate for your child, in case people ask.

- Include in your reading sessions and play sessions stories about giving and receiving presents. That way you can rehearse appropriate responses.

- If paper ripping is a big 'thing' for your child, check that the parcel doesn't contain something that might get damaged and let him enjoy it!

- Don't overdo the big 'Santa' build-up. The concept of a strange man visiting the house can create a lot of anxiety. Try to shield your child a little from too much Santa talk and explain to siblings why they should too if possible.

As props to help you interact, toys can be incredibly useful or can cause untold frustration and upset or simply be ignored. Choosing carefully, structuring carefully and planning carefully will help you extract the most from the equipment you already have.

Chapter 5

Table-Top Games and Puzzles

What is a puzzle?
The word 'puzzle' might be described as anything that makes your child *think* – an activity with a clear set of actions, which is prompted by yourself, that has a solution. Puzzles can be problematic to children with autism for a variety of reasons other than the difficulty of the actual puzzle itself. This type of activity requires:

- direction from an adult
- co-operation from the child to observe and follow instruction
- motivation to actually do the activity.

To non-autistic children none of the above are usually a problem, and the delight at completing a puzzle (with the associated praise and attention), is reward in itself, which fuels motivation to try again and move on. For children on the autism spectrum, all of the above can get in the way of playing and consequently of learning. Such children do not learn incidentally by exploring and trying new ideas throughout the day; rigid patterns of thinking, behaviour and speech mean they often resist participating in an activity that requires *joint attention* to a problem and *flexible* thinking to solve it.

There are, however, some attractive qualities that puzzles have to children with autism which can be harnessed to aid learning and interaction:

- Puzzle play is predictable – there is only one right conclusion that can be repeated over and over again.

- Puzzle play is visual, whether it is completing a jigsaw or sorting picture cards. Children with autism are often well tuned into their visual channel.

One aid to learning through this type of puzzle play is *structure*. Structuring play is a recurring theme throughout the book and is as appropriate to activities such as reading and drawing as it is to solving puzzles and joint playing. For more information on structuring play and breaking down an activity into its separate tasks, see Chapter 3. Many of the activities below can also be used for the early learning 'work box' activities, also described in Chapter 3.

For this type of play, remember to:

- confine the work area to a specific place – preferably a table at which you can both sit

- use a picture prompt to communicate to and 'cue' your child about which activity you will be doing and another to explain that there will be a reward or break at the end

- keep instructions very clear and simple – try not to overload your child with simultaneous verbal instructions and physical gestures

- only request that your child co-operates for very short periods at a time.

If your child finds the directness of this approach too uncomfortable, go back to indirect play techniques, for example, have the same task set up in front of each of you and complete your task as if for your own pleasure. Draw your child's attention to what you are doing by using the techniques to gain attention detailed in Chapter 2. Then slowly introduce very short bursts of directed play as follows.

Getting started

Even though you may feel your child's abilities stretch way beyond the task, if this is the first time you are introducing table-top structured play, start with a *very* simple task that purely requires your child to follow your direction – something stressful and uncomfortable for children with autism, which is why initial sessions should be kept short.

☺   Place a small container (cup, box etc.) in the middle of the table and an object like a plastic toy in front of your child and ask him first to look at you (which is a demanding enough request to a child who finds eye contact distressing) and then to put the toy in the box. It might go something like this:

Mum: 'Charlie look at Mummy…'

(After a few requests Charlie makes eye contact for a couple of seconds.)

Mum: 'Well done, Charlie. Put duck in box Charlie…'

(Charlie ignores the request and starts to get up and walk away. Mum physically guides him back to the chair. Put duck in box Charlie and *then* tickles…", (Charlie loves being tickled).

(Mum shows the following pictures to Charlie.)

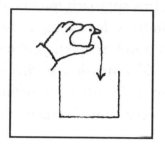 

(Mum then gently holds Charlie's hand and closes it over the duck, moves it to the box and drops it in, saying)

Mum: "Yes, well done… Charlie put duck in box."

Immediately Charlie gets out of the chair and Mum has a good tickling, rough-and-tumble play session with him. In subsequent sessions the game is kept as entertaining as possible – Mum makes the duck 'swim' across the table and make a loud 'quack' as it goes in the box. Although much of Charlie's play is based on Mum tuning into *his* activities on his terms in order to encourage his awareness of her, she feels that short bursts of structured table-top play like this help to encourage him to follow instruction, help his ability to process and understand language and work on his aversion to being directed.

☺   Your child might prefer to do an activity like this in a way that has more meaning to him, for example, put a spoon in a cup, put the biscuit on the plate, the pencil in the box, etc.

Although this is an exercise in teaching your child to listen and follow an instruction it doesn't have to be a battle of wills. Remind yourself that this seemingly very simple activity is actually demanding a lot of your child by making him resist his brain's natural motivation to avoid. Make the activity into a game and inject some fun into it: bring the objects to life, or try using a glove puppet to demonstrate the action first. Glove puppets are useful aids for all sorts of interaction – they remove some of the stress of direct confrontation (acting almost like a third party).

Prompting eye contact is important, even though your child might find it uncomfortable. By being able to look at you, he can see what you might be holding for him to look at, see you showing him what to do and can register your expression. All children on the autism spectrum have difficulty making and maintaining eye contact but the degree of difficulty varies greatly from one child to the next. Two seconds may be a momentous achievement for one child or easily done for another child.

Try the following ideas, tailoring them to your own child's attention span and special interests:

Shapes

☺ Materials

- Small plastic bucket or box.
- Two wooden or plastic shapes (circle/square).

Instruction
'Put circle in bucket'. After a time, add more choice of shapes until you feel your child is consistently discriminating between them. Add some variety by saying, 'Give Mummy triangle' or 'Point to oblong'. Keep your language as simple as possible; add words like 'the' when you think your child is ready.

☺ Materials

- Inset jigsaw with 'shape' pieces.

Instructions
Hold two shapes up in front of your face and say, 'Which shape?' Try to get your child to say which shape he wants or point to which shape. This helps to make the activity more

interactive than simply placing all the shapes into the puzzle. It also gives opportunity to reinforce the names of the shapes.

☺   **Materials**

- Two sets of four picture cards of shapes (i.e. two circles, two squares, two triangles, two oblongs). You could try drawing these yourself – make a set in simple black outline first so that your child doesn't confuse the labels for shapes and colours.

Instructions

Put one card (for example, a circle) on the table in front of your child and hold up a matching card plus one other (for example, a circle and a square). Pointing to the card on the table ask your child, 'Which is the same?' When he points to the correct card, place them side by side saying, "Look circle, circle – the same!" You can also try this matching game with a variety of picture cards – try 'animal snap' cards or a TV character that your child is familiar with.

☺   **Materials**

- A button, a square coaster, a cheese triangle or other household items that have a specific shape.
- A set of line drawings: circle, square triangle etc.

Instructions

Place the line drawings on the table and hand the items to your child one by one saying, 'What shape is button?' Guide your child's hand to the correct line drawing and place the item on top saying, for example, 'Yes, button is a circle shape!'

☺   **Materials**

- Shape sorter – try the type that responds with a pleasing sound or flashing lights (see references at the back of the book).

Instructions

Hold two shapes up in front of your face and ask your child to either point to or say which shape he wants. To start of with you will have to keep telling him, for example, 'Which shape – circle or square?' Be aware if he simply repeats your last word every time. If this happens say, 'Point to shape you want?' When he has pointed, then repeat, 'Tom wants the circle'. Use your child's name in the instructions.

Introducing fun into table-top play

Children with autism differ in how much encouragement and excitement they enjoy. When an activity is completed correctly, the sound of your delighted voice might actually be uncomfortable for your child; another child may relish his parent's pleasure at his behaviour. Judge your own child. If he enjoys praise, let him know consistently how pleased you are – clap, hug, do a dance! If he appears to not enjoy too much excited praise then show your pleasure in a different way; keep your voice quiet but make the items he's just worked with jump up and down on the table – keep the play fresh, energetic and enjoyable.

If it looks like a particular activity such as learning shapes is uninteresting to your child, then move the play off the table top and try a totally new approach, for example:

☺   Stick drawings of different shapes onto large cushions and play a 'ready, steady, go' game, whereby your child has to jump onto the correct cushion. This can also be done for colours, objects etc.

☺   Try using an obsessional activity such as spinning to create a learning element. One lady who responded to my survey had taught her son his colours by painting them on jam-jar lids for him to spin. You might for example have three spinners or lids with different shapes on and request him to spin a particular shape or make a big spinner from a hexagon of card with a pencil through the middle. On each side of the hexagon draw a shape and let your child spin. When the spinner stops and falls on a particular side look at the shape it has landed on and match it to its picture card.

☺   Draw a grid on a large piece of paper and draw a shape in each square of the grid. Let your child spin a small top over it, encourage your child to point to or say the shape that the spinner lands on.

☺   Look at what activities your child indulges in and see if you can add a learning element, whereby a solitary activity can be brought to a table top or specific play area and used as part of a structured and interactive play session. For example, for 'paper rippers' put three pieces of paper with a shape drawn on each and request your child rips a specific shape, for example, 'Helen rip the triangle.'

☺   Try presenting the activity in a small box – a fancy gift box is ideal. This gives your child time to anticipate that the activity will follow. At the end of the activity your child can have the pleasure of putting all the pieces back into the box and putting the lid on – using containers in this way can be very appealing to some children. The procedure of putting the items away and back in the box is also a signal to your child that the particular activity has come to an end.

Colours

You can use all the above ideas for colours. Don't forget to look at the games and activities your child already has and just use some of the elements. Also try the following:

☺ **Materials**

- Four primary-coloured plastic balls.

- Clear rigid plastic (for example, heavy weight acetate) folded into a tube and secured with tape.

Attach the plastic tube upright into a shoe box with a hole cut in the lid as follows:

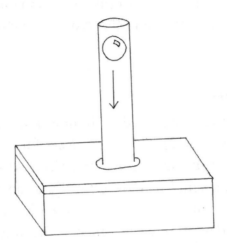

Instructions

Hold up two balls in front of your child and ask which he wants to put in the tube. When he points, encourage him to label the colour. Also try lining the balls in front of your child and requesting a specific colour. As he begins to understand the labels, try a sequence, for example, 'red then yellow'. Use physical prompts where necessary, for example, tapping the table next to the correct ball, or touching his shoulder to encourage him to choose. Try to keep verbal prompts to a minimum so that your child doesn't come to rely on them and doesn't overload, processing too much language.

☺ Use a set of stacking rings to teach colours. Sets like this can have more of a reward for your child if they light up or play tunes. Look through the baby sections in toy shops and try the manufacturers at the back of this book. Toys such as these are more expensive than their basic counterparts but often have that extra appeal to motivate a child whose attention is difficult to hold. Don't be afraid to use 'baby toys' in your table-top play. They often have great 'cause and effect' appeal.

☺   *Letters and numbers* – If you feel your child is ready, there are lots of ideas in Chapter 14 (in the section on early literacy skills) that can be adapted to this type of structured table-top play.

Matching games

Matching games can be played with almost anything – pictures, toys, real objects – though it will be easier for your child to start matching objects to pictures rather than pictures to pictures at first. Encouraging your child to look critically at an object to assess where to put it means he can begin to work out the visual and functional differences between objects (the way a non-autistic child would by asking questions). It also gives you lots of opportunity to repeat the verbal label for an object and for your child to associate the sound with how it looks and feels in his hand. These activities utilise his visual thinking skills to help him learn.

Try the following:

☺   **Matching real objects to pictures**

Materials
A pack of good quality photo cards from a special educational needs supplier is a good investment (see back of book for details). Alternatively, a less expensive option is to purchase a 'baby's first words' photo style book and cut the pictures out and stick them onto card. For example, you might have photos

of a banana, a cotton reel, a teacup, a pencil and a matching set of real objects, i.e. banana, cotton reel etc.

Instructions

Place the four picture cards in front of your child and hand him the objects one by one, asking him to 'find the same'. Prompt your child to place the real objects onto their matching pictures. Label each item as he does it. To add extra appeal, try pulling the items out of a bag and adding a surprise element, for example, 'What's coming next? It's a pencil!' You might even set up four boxes with the photos attached to the side of each box. Your child then has the satisfaction of placing its matching object into the box.

☺   Matching toy objects to pictures

Try a similar game with photo cards and their toy counterparts, for example, tractor, farm/zoo animals, ball, book etc., or put three photos of *your own* car, pet, house on the table in front of your child and three equivalent toys (car, dog/cat, house). Ask your child to 'find same', and give him the toys one at a time to match to their appropriate cards.

☺   Matching pictures to pictures

Finally, using a variety of pictures of the same thing, encourage your child to match pictures from magazines etc. to their photo cards. To give this game appeal, stick the magazine pictures onto different coloured cards and place them face down, with the photo cards facing upwards in a row above them. If your child knows his colours you could ask him to choose a colour, turn it over and match, or you might just fan them out in front of him and encourage him to choose one. Remember you could introduce any objects that have a special appeal in your pictures.

☺   **Hot Dots Power Pen**

The Hot Dots Power Pen (by Educational Insights – see back of book for details) is an electronic apparatus, held like a pen, that rewards a correct answer with fun sounds and flashing lights when it is pressed onto the appropriate dot. The pen can be bought as a package with ready prepared lessons featuring shapes, colours etc., or you can purchase packs of dots and make your own. By making your own you can keep the activity as simple as you like. For example, you could prepare one of the cards as follows:

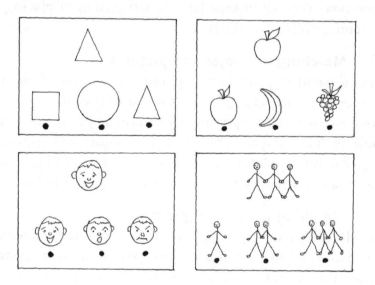

When your child presses the pen onto the matching dot he is rewarded with lights and sounds – wrong dots give a simple 'wrong' sound. This type of aid removes some of your direction by being self-correcting and has its own reward, motivating your child to attempt the activity. You can also specifically tailor the activity to your child's ability and interest, so it is a good investment (though needs reasonably good hand/eye co-ordination).

Posting games

If you spend a little time creating a posting box out of a shoe box (covered in paper or painted), you will have an invaluable item that can be used time and again for a variety of activities. Remember not to seal the sides as you need the lid to be removable to retrieve items.

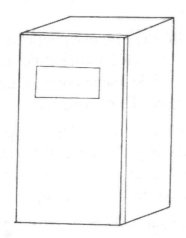

Try the following:

☺ **Materials**

A set of picture cards – tailor your choice to your child's ability level. There are many such sets of pictures available from specialist catalogues and some toy stores (snap cards can also be useful). Don't forget to ask your child's speech and language therapist if there are any materials that can be lent out; also check out special needs toy libraries.

Themed sets include:

- verbs
- nouns
- opposites
- prepositions

- actions
- body parts.

Instructions

Only present two or three cards (from the same pack) at a time until your child becomes skilled at the activity. Ask your child to, for example, "post cup". Keep up motivation with fresh ideas, for example:

- Let your child wear a glove puppet to do the posting – or wear one yourself for your child to hand the picture to. Add fun – make the puppet eat the card or run off with it and generally be naughty!

- When looking at actions – for example, walking, hopping, jumping – have a doll or teddy on the table to demonstrate the action (your child might be too distracted if *you* get up and do it).

- When looking at body parts, have a mirror to hand to look at faces, or pat the appropriate part on each other.

Simple jigsaws

☺   The simplest jigsaw puzzle consists of one picture split down the centre, or with a corner removed. Stick a photograph or picture of a favourite character onto stiff card and cut off a corner. Place them in front of your child on the table and say, 'Sam do it' – physically prompt him if necessary to place the pieces together.

☺   Jigsaw puzzles where the pieces fit into a wooden board and often have a little knob for your child to grasp are satisfying – they have a definite fit and are not as frustrating as regular jigsaw puzzles. Again, hold up the pieces two at a time in front of your face and let your child choose which piece he wants to fit in – make him aware of *your* involvement in the activity.

☺   When your child is ready to move on to regular jigsaws, choose a picture/scene you feel he might find appealing and one that doesn't have too much fussy visual detail to take in. Again, work on a table top or flat area where the pieces will fit properly and lie flat. There is a procedure called 'back chaining', which simply means letting your child complete the last piece and then the last *two* pieces etc. after you have first made up the puzzle. When you have completed the jigsaw, ask your child to point to elements in the picture – guide his hand with yours if necessary. If your child is totally uninterested in puzzles, try leaving out a completed puzzle with one piece out. It is likely that during the course of the day he will fit in the last piece, the next day leave out two pieces. After three or four days return the puzzle to the table top and see if he will tolerate a joint session putting the puzzle together.

Bricks

Free play with bricks can be problematic for a variety of reasons:

- Multiple pieces can be used in repetitive and rigid ways – stacking, lining up, etc.

- Using bricks imaginatively and creatively is very difficult for children whose imaginations are significantly impaired.

- Bricks that click together can frustrate a child who doesn't have the fine motor skills to do this. For a child who can manage, the fact that his tower will not extend forever and will eventually become top heavy and fall over may also cause frustration and distress. For this reason, good size blocks may be a better option: they sit on top of each other in a less specific way than bricks and have the added advantage that you can use them with your child to create an opportunity for him to communicate to you by building towers for him to knock over in a 'ready...steady...(long pause for your child to communicate)...go' game

Teaching your child to play flexibly and imaginatively with bricks and blocks may be done as part of a structured table-top play session. Try the following :

☺   Arrange four or five pieces in front of your child and give yourself a collection of the same blocks. Keep your areas separate by having a piece of card or a tray each to build on. Try demonstrating a simple house by placing a triangle on top of a rectangle. It might help to draw a very simple house on paper, then to point to the bricks and back at the drawing saying, "A house, look Tom". Work on a collection of around three separate elements – house, tree, bridge – then try adding some figures.

Threading

Threading is great practice for underdeveloped fine motor skills. Unfortunately, a lot of the threading activities available in shops have small parts and are difficult to get to grips with. Try making your own as follows:

☺   Attach a thin piece of dowelling, approximately 15 cm tall and about the width of a pencil (or even thinner), to a base board.

Take this with you when you go to purchase wooden beads (from a craft/sewing shop) to check that they fit on easily. Make up a series of picture cards illustrating the shape or colour order in which they are to be threaded (start with an easy one of one/two beads and gradually add more). Place the card in front of your child and prompt him through the order they are to be threaded.

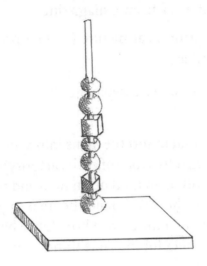

When he has mastered this try moving on to a thick shoelace with the end bound in tape to make it rigid. Add variety by threading cotton reels, large buttons, sweets, cereals, pasta, straws to make belts and necklaces.

Categories

Because of the generalization problems that children with autism have, it is important to make sure that just because your child understands a label from one picture that he can use this consistently whether he sees for example a cow in real life, a plastic cow, a furry cow, a photo of a cow etc. Try setting up the following:

☺ Materials

Two empty shoe boxes and a collection of objects each representing two different things, for example, house and car. Your objects might include the following:

- A toy car.

- A photo of your own car.

- A picture of a car from a magazine.

- A stylised cartoon car picture (from a packet of snap cards or similar).

Plus a similar set of objects depicting 'house'.

Instructions

Encourage your child to sort the items into a 'house' box and a 'car' box. Put the first two (one of each category) into the boxes to start the game off, then hold up an item and pointing to the boxes say, "Cow or house?". Hand the item to your child and prompt him to put it in the correct box. Once he gets the hang of generalizing images for the same thing, you might try some simple categories:

- animals

- people

- transport

- food

- flowers.

You can find images on old greeting cards, magazines, comics, photos. Stick them onto card so that they are robust and your child isn't distracted by what may be printed on the reverse. Gradually you will find you have a collection of images that can be used for many different games and activities. Try filing them in a simple folder so that you can access them quickly next time you need them.

☺   Add variety to your categorization games. Vary where your child puts the objects, for example, boxes, buckets, handbags. Try a categorization game for birds and animals, with a cardboard tree laid flat for your child to put pictures of birds on and a green cardboard field for animals. During the course of the day, if your child likes to imitate you doing household chores, do simple sorting with the cutlery or putting washing into light and dark piles.

☺ Memory Games

Materials

- Two identical plastic cups
- Something your child will be motivated to find, for example, a chocolate.

Instructions

Place the two cups in front of your child and put the chocolate underneath one of them in front of him. Slowly and deliberately swap the cups round and encourage him to point to the one with the chocolate underneath. Try adding an extra cup but only make one or two switches very slowly. When he's consistently tracking the cup with the chocolate in, try moving on to memory games with pictures. Familiar photos would be a good place to start.

Place two photos face down in front of your child and show him what each picture is first, 'This is Daddy and this is Simon…give me Daddy.' Once you are sure your child recognizes all the pictures, try turning them face down (two or three at a time) and then asking the same questions.

All of the table-top games and puzzles are great activities to use in your 'structured early learning sessions', detailed in Chapter 3. You might try choosing two or three activities to use in one session followed by a reward/reinforcer. There are plenty of ideas for re-inforcers in Chapter 4 – these can be anything from the obvious edible treat to obsessional activities, social rewards such as tickles, bubbles, rough-and-tumble or attractive objects, such as glitter, bubble tubes or spinning tops, that your child wants to see or use. Remember to communicate which reward is coming after the activity by drawing a simple picture of it and using it as a picture prompt.

Bear in mind that (as with all the suggestions in the book) the above are 'ideas' for you to choose from not a list of activities where each needs to be done before you can move on to the next one. Choose an activity pitched at your child's level of ability and readiness to follow your direction and only ask him to join you in this structured table-top play for very short burst of a few minutes at a time.

Remember that even though table-top puzzle play is more formal than other types of playing it should still be *fun* enough to encourage motivation. As parents anxious for our children to interact it's easy to get frustrated if the child cannot follow our instructions to perform the simplest of tasks, yet left to his own devises can line up items in order of decreasing size with great precision, or skillfully balance a collection of toys. The moment playing becomes forced and tense it's time to stop, rethink and lighten up!

Chapter 6

Music

Saviour and enemy

For children with autism, the sound sensitivities that many have can make music both a saviour (to block out other distressing noises) and an enemy (when thrust upon a child unexpectedly). Most of the parents who responded to my 'autism and play' survey commented that listening to music was an important part of their child's day; however, problems often occurred when children became fixated on certain songs, constantly wore headphones or hummed tunes repeatedly.

In fact, all responses to questions on music indicated that it had an 'effect': either that the child loved it to the point of obsession or was affected by it, though not necessarily positively. My own son has gone through phases of repeating the same tape over and over (particularly at bedtime or when stressed). When he was a toddler, if we forgot to take a tape player on trips with us there was a price to pay and playing the wrong tape or starting it at a different point created an extreme reaction. However, for the first three years of his life the tape of nursery rhymes had a greater soothing effect on him than any amount of attention from me and became an indispensable part of our lives.

Why music can be an enemy

Auditory processing problems (which appear to affect all children with autism to varying degrees), mean that sounds that cannot be anticipated, have never been heard before, or are unexpectedly loud can cause an immediate anxiety state – screaming, running away from the source of the noise, covering ears etc. With music, unanticipated sounds can also cause similar reactions, often resulting in the child attempting to turn off or break the player or refusing to enter a room where music is playing. Conversely, but still negatively, music can become an obsessive and repetitive activity that aids children with autism to withdraw. The very comfort of a familiar tune can satisfy a craving for sameness that takes the child beyond relaxation and into a state of 'tuned out' aloneness. It may even be that despite his best efforts the child simply cannot get songs out of his head by rediverting his focus of attention. Try reading *The Self Help Guide for Special Kids and Their Parents*, written by the then eleven-year-old James Williams, for an eloquent account of how this feels (for further details see the references at the back of this book).

Why music can be a saviour

When a song or piece of music is comfortable and familiar but does not satisfy a need for ritual, the child is in control and the music can be used to block out other distracting sounds or sensations and actually help him calm down and concentrate. A number of parents in the survey reported that at varying times their children had used listening to music through headphones as a way to help them concentrate on other things such as homework. For children who have a problem processing competing sensory information this seems like a contradiction; however, anecdotally, this does seem to be the case. I myself have worked in the past with two autistic adults who were better able to concentrate (as well as take instructions from me), when wearing headphones playing music (at a moderately low volume). This worked for these individuals – for others it might just render them incapable of *any* interaction.

Somewhere between the two positive and negative extremes is a way to use the predictability, rhythm and comfort of musical sounds positively.

Music therapy for children (and adults) with autism is becoming increasingly recognised as a way to encourage interaction and social awareness as well as a useful tool for relaxation. If you want more information on where to find a qualified music therapist in your area, contact:

The British Society for Music Therapy (BSMT)
25 Rosslyn Avenue, East Barnet, Hertfordshire. EN4 8DH
Tel and Fax: 020 8368 8879
Email: info@bsmt.org
Website: *www.bsmt.org*

Ideas to try at home

Before embarking on the following ideas be aware of your child's individual sensitivities to sound – keep the volume and length of activity within a comfortable zone. Your child may enjoy music but need a scarf wrapped over his ears or ear plugs to make it more comfortable to listen to. Headphones (without the flex attached) can also lessen the sound intensity until your child becomes used to it. (They are also useful if sound levels out and about at home or in school are getting uncomfortably loud.)

Finding a collection of enjoyable pieces

You may already know your child's favourite music or he may rigidly have a few tracks that he will tolerate. Use these at first but try to build in flexibility. It may be unbearable for him to listen to a new a piece of music coming out of the same player on which he only plays one comforting track. To introduce new sounds, change the context – the car, the radio, a different tape player. Play music in the garden or the bath – places he doesn't normally listen to it and with which he hasn't developed an association. Experiment with a number of different styles – pop, classical, folk, new age, brass band, musical sound tracks – and be aware of which ones produce a favorable response. For each piece try creating a picture symbol (for example, a drum, trumpet, singing face). For obscure music try something like a rainbow – anything visual that your child can associate with that *particular* piece of music. Stick a copy of the symbol on the tape box/CD cover and keep a second copy of the picture to communicate to your child which piece of music is about to be played. You can either just show your child the picture, saying, 'Music now', or use it as part of a picture timetable (see Chapter 3, 'Structured Play').

Listening and playing to music together

☺   Young children with autism often love swinging and dancing whilst being carried by an adult and will tolerate a level of physical closeness in this situation that they might normally find uncomfortable. Hold your child at eye level and try to maintain eye contact for a few seconds at a time whilst you sway – this can be a lovely experience of closeness. Don't forget to stop for pauses and build in anticipation before you commence again.

☺   Sit opposite your child with your legs over each other's and pull him forwards and back in a rocking motion to the music – remember to put a cushion on the floor behind him in case he throws his head back! Build in lots of anticipation, especially if you sing a rhyme such as 'Row row row your boat'.

☺   Lie on your back and put your bare feet against your child's – follow what he does with his feet first and then try to get him to move his in time with yours. This can be done with hands too.

☺   Let your child stand on *your* feet, facing you whilst you hold him round the chest and dance.

☺   If your child likes fluttery bits of paper or ribbon, try tying lengths of ribbon or streamers to garden canes (sand the ends smooth) and wave them to the music, or tie chiffon scarves to hands.

☺   Try simple exercises to music. Choose a slow gentle piece or a rhythmic nursery rhyme. Lie your child on his back and lift his arms up, slowly placing them back down on the floor above his head. Place a rolled-up towel under the hollow of his back, this will help him open his lungs, breath deeply and relax, repeat half a dozen times or as long as is comfortable. Try moving his legs whilst saying, 'Out, in, up and down' in rhythm to the music. Build up the anticipation of a movement and then leave a long pause to create an opportunity for him to make a gesture or noise that he wants the game to continue. Remember the point of this is not to exercise your child's limbs (although this does have its own benefits) but to make him aware of rhythm, timing and more importantly of *you*.

Relaxation

Learning to relax is essential for children with autism. It gives them a tool for later life for keeping in control of the frustrations and anxiety that thinking, understanding and feeling differently to the rest of the people on the planet can cause. Music can be a great help in introducing relaxation skills.

☺   Lie your child on his back and roll him side to side. He may prefer you to sit behind him rather than face to face, or rock him in an orthopaedic, 'v'-shaped pillow. Try this after a bout of distress/anger/tantrums or when he's displaying signs of anxiety.

☺   Massage your child to the music. Take his lead – some children like a strong purposeful touch, others might find this invasive. If your child enjoys it try attending a massage class to learn how to do this safely, or talk to your occupational therapy department about sensory integration techniques.

☺   Rub talc or cream into his hands and feet in time to the rhythm of the music as a soothing pre-bedtime activity. Your child might like to do this to you too – ignore the mess and enjoy the togetherness! Try some of the 'relaxation' music collections such as sounds of nature, but be aware of any sounds that your child finds uncomfortable.

Scripts to rhythm – encouraging speech through song

Using music, in this context, does not simply mean playing set pieces on tapes/CDs; it can mean anything from tapping drum beats to clapping in time to speech to 'singing' speech. Normal speech has a sense of rhythm and timing which even high-functioning and verbal children with autism find difficult – making them socially clumsy in adult life. Using rhythm to play games with such children can help on many levels, for example:

- Exaggerating the rhythm and intonation of speech can make children with autism more aware of when a sentence starts and stops, and the novelty of rhythmic language seems to make it easier for them to attend to the content.

- The lack of early motivation to interact means many autistic children have missed out on learning pre-verbal skills such as 'social turn-taking', making conversational turn-taking problematic. Often, verbal children on the autism spectrum will deliver monologues of speech without waiting for responses or attending to what the other person wants to say. Synchronizing your speech to the rhythm of your child's movements makes him aware of how his actions can change the speed/content of your speech and may draw him into a joint activity.

How does this work in practice? – ideas

As with many of the ideas in this book you will have to drop some of your inhibitions about appropriate ways of relating to your child – after a while you will find a way of singing commentaries, freely and spontaneously, to capitalize on situations as they arise.

☺ There are many everyday situations that you can start singing commentaries to your child about for example, getting dressed, washing, brushing teeth, hair, eating, swinging, sliding.

If your child isn't used to you singing to him, start off gently in a low tone voice – maybe only one or two times in the day. If you find it hard to make things up on the spot, jot some ideas down in the late evening, in the bath, whilst ironing – whenever you have five minutes to think. Try to include:

- some simple rhymes (though this isn't a test of poetry skills!)
- repetition
- your child's name

- the action your child is doing

- simple language.

You don't need to stick to a particular tune – make it up as you go along – but to start off with you might like to use familiar nursery tunes such as 'Twinkle, twinkle little star' or 'London bridge is falling down'. Here are some examples:

(To the tune of, 'Twinkle, twinkle…')

Thomas, Thomas, brush your teeth
Thomas, Thomas, make them clean
Brush them, brush them, make them white
Brush them, brush them, clean and bright
Thomas, Thomas, brush your teeth
Thomas, Thomas, make them clean.

(To the tune of 'Incy, wincy spider')

Lucy Lucy Lucy
It's nearly time for tea
Lucy Lucy Lucy
Sit down with me
We'll eat up all the food
Until it's all gone
Lucy Lucy Lucy
Eating tea – yum yum!

(To the tune of 'Row, row, row, your boat')

Brush, brush, brush Jane's hair
Make it shine and shine
Gently, gently, gently, gently
Now it's looking fine.

Here's some you could sing to your own tunes:

Dressing

(Use lots of enthusiasm, shaking and nodding head etc.)

Let's get dressed, Jack, let's get dressed
Here's your pants and here's your vest
One leg, two legs, in they go
Are we ready? …(pause)…not yet, no!
Let's get dressed, Jack, let's get dressed
Here's your trousers, here's your shirt
Two legs, two arms, in they go
Are we ready? …(pause)…not yet, no!
Let's get dressed, Jack, let's get dressed
Here's your socks and here's your shoes
Left foot, right foot, can you guess?
Are we ready? …(pause)…yes, yes, yes!

Pointing

This rhyme can help with the problem of understanding pronouns (I, me, you etc.)

I can see the window
Can you see it too?
I can point like this
Now it's time for…you! (Mould your child's fingers into a point if necessary)
Pointing to the window
There it is, see
Pointing to the window
Sally and me (point to your child and then yourself).

You can add lots of subsequent verses using the same formula, for example, 'I can see the ceiling/clouds/trees' etc.)

Here's one for comforting a distressed child (rather than bombarding them with 'What's wrong?', 'What have you done?' etc.)

Sad, sad boy, come here to me
Don't cry now, sit on my knee
Sad, sad boy, be calm, calm, calm
Feeling calm now in my arms

Calm, calm boy, come here to me
Sitting still now on my knee
Calm, calm boy, get happy now
Feeling happy in my arms

Happy boy, happy boy, come here to me
Smiling now sit on my knee
Happy boy let's smile, smile, smile
Have a cuddle and we'll play in a while.

Don't forget to use ordinary nursery rhymes to encourage interaction. Rhymes such as 'Round and round the garden like a teddy bear, one step, two steps…tickle you under there!' have a built-in pause and motivation to encourage your child to either finish the rhyme or communicate non-verbally through eye contact, sounds or gestures that he wants it to continue.

Singing spontaneous commentaries

After a session of structured play, your child is probably going to have a break – some free time to do his own thing – even if this is just moving randomly around the room, pacing in lines or flicking paper. After what you feel is a long enough break without interaction, try to regain his attention by singing a commentary about what he is doing. When I use the word 'singing' this may only be a rhythmic chant or a song to a familiar or made up tune. Again keep it slow, simple and repetitive. For example:

William's running to the door, run run run,
Knocking tap tap tap, tapping on the door
William's jumping off the sofa one, two, three,
William's on the floor now looking at me
Ellen's looking at the sky blue blue sky, listen listen listen
Ellen hears a bird, cheep cheep cheep
Then the bird flies away!
John is rocking rocking rocking, forwards back forwards back
Squish goes the bean bag, squish squish squish
Now John's clapping clap clap clap
Faster faster faster clappety clappety clap.

You can make a commentary about absolutely anything. Initially your child might ignore you, but is likely to become aware at some point that his movements and actions are affecting the rhythm and content of what you are saying. He might start deliberately moving fast to see what happens, or stopping still completely to see if the commentary will stop (which of course it will!). He might start humming or repeating your words but what is happening all the time is his solitary autistic 'aloneness' is being turned into a more joint activity – again one in which what you say and do is meaningful in *relation* to what he is doing.

☺   Vary the speed and rhythm of your commentary to your child's actions – fast, high voices for rapid movements; low, slow speech for slow movements.

☺   Stop the commentary abruptly the minute your child is completely still. This can become a game in itself, almost like a version of musical statues.

☺   Try accompanying the commentary with a simple instrument – a chime bar or wooden block – but keep the instrument quiet enough that your child can hear your words.

☺   Don't give up too early – it may take your child five minutes to realize what you are doing. Likewise, if the session goes on too long and your child is showing signs of irritation, stop.

Making your own music

Throughout the book I make references to 'themed play boxes', anything from a box of novelties and knick knacks to gain attention (Chapter 2) to collections of items to create imaginative play sequences (Chapter 13). Likewise, it is useful to have a *music box* consisting of both shop-bought and home-made instruments preferably in 'twos' – one for you and one for your child or in threes or fours if your child prefers to hold one in each hand.

Suggestions for items to go in your music box:

- Tambourine
- Bazooka
- Bells
- Drum
- Castanets
- Children's keyboard (these are relatively inexpensive for a very simple one)
- Plastic flute
- Rainmaker
- Party blowers

Robust and unusual instruments make great suggestions for relatives and friends who are stuck for gift ideas! See the back of this book for suppliers of children's instruments.

Items to make

- Blocks of wood with sandpaper on one side that can be rubbed together.

- Pots of all shapes and sizes can be used like drums when struck with a wooden spoon.

- Older children may like the sound of empty milk bottles filled with water (a collection of different levels to make different notes).

- Maraca-style instruments can be made from a variety of materials to make different sounds – remember to seal the join between the lid and the rest of the container with parcel tape. Try some of the following containers:
    - plastic milk cartons
    - metal coffee tin
    - small shoe box
    - plastic powdered drinks jar
    - milk shake powder box.

    Possible fillings:
    - sand
    - dried peas/beans/lentils
    - buttons
    - rice
    - dried pasta.

Using your music box

Imitation

Learning to imitate is a vital skill that most parents take for granted unless their child for some reason cannot or will not imitate sounds or actions. Children with autism have fundamental problems with imitation. Many of the activities in this book are based around breaking play skills down so that your child is only required to imitate one action at a time. Musical sounds are a good basis for teaching imitation – the sounds are often a reward in themselves that help to motivate children to follow direction. Try the following:

☺   After indicating to your child that it's time to play with musical instruments (either verbally or with a picture prompt), place two instruments (the same ones) in front of you and your child, for example, a tambourine each. When your child picks up the instrument try to copy every sound he makes with it. Make your child aware that you are copying him; try to maintain eye contact in short bursts, and look like you are thinking about what sound he has made. If necessary, enlist the help of another adult to help him make a specific sound, for example, three taps on the tambourine, the adult could then say something like, 'Mummy's turn now' and direct your child's attention to you doing three taps on the tambourine. Once your child gets the hang of the fact that *you* are copying *him*, see if he will copy you (again the help of a second adult may be useful to prompt him). Bazookas are good for this as you can hum a familiar tune or very specific notes. Drums are good for producing distinct loud and quiet bangs for your child to copy. You might then move on to encouraging your child to listen to a rhythm and imitate it – keep it very simple at first, possibly a familiar rhythm such as a nursery rhyme.

☺   If your child enjoys his own vocal sounds try an 'echo mike' – have one to use yourself and copy his vocalizations. Be responsive to any attempts he makes to copy some of your own sounds.

☺   Try leaving out two instruments during the course of the day and if he picks one up and starts to use it, be ready to jump in there and start copying him! Or begin to play simply for your own pleasure and observe what your child does.

Listening Games

Learning to listen is a valuable skill (for both verbal and nonverbal children with autism) that can be improved through these types of exercises. Remember during the course of the day to point out sounds for your child to listen to – dripping taps, rain on roofs, crackling fires etc.

As part of your structured music session try the following game:

☺   When your child is used to some structured table-top learning (as detailed in Chapters 3 and 5) try setting up a screen between yourself and your child on a table top – this can be a simple piece of heavy duty card with the side bent so that it will support itself upright or you might decide to make something more robust out of wood. Set the table top up as shown:

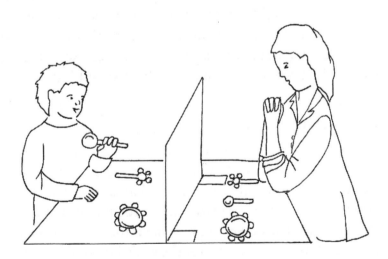

Start by making a sound with one instrument and asking your child to listen and copy with his own – you may need to enlist the help of a second adult to prompt him to listen and choose. When your child chooses and responds correctly, give him lots of positive feedback – show him your instrument so that he can see he has used the same one (or not if that is the case). When he starts to get the hang of listening for one sound, try doing two and then three in a row and seeing if he will copy a sequence of sounds. Finally, prompt your child to choose a sound for you to copy and steer the activity into a turn-taking game.

☺   *Sound lotto (bingo)* – These games work by providing you with a number of lotto boards and a tape of sounds – everyday sounds, animal sounds etc. To start with use just one board. This may mean making your own edited version of the tape by re-taping only the sounds that appear on that one board. (If your child has to listen to a dozen different sounds before he spots one on his board he may rapidly lose concentration.) Your child places a coloured counter on each picture when he hears its associated sound on the tape. Instead of the coloured counters, you might want to make a photocopy of the board and cut out the nine individual pictures so that he can match them to the board pictures as he listens to each sound. See the back of the book for where to purchase sound lotto games.

☺   *Musical bumps* – 'Stop/start' listening games have a good element of physical fun and are great for siblings and friends to join in with. Start with the simplest version – musical bumps. You may need to do lots of prompting and encouragement at first to help your child understand what is expected. There is no need for him to dance to the music; you might simply swing arms or stand. The object of the game is for him to listen to the music and note when it stops by sitting down. Also try providing your child with a keyboard or drum (again a second adult may be useful). Encourage him to play randomly while *you* dance. Helped by a second adult your child then stops playing and you have to freeze very still. Make this fun for your child – pretend to wobble, stand on one leg, get the giggles. Let him see that the reason you are doing this whole playing thing is because it is *fun*!

☺   You could try a very simple stop/start game using one of the novelty greeting cards that plays a tune when opened and stops when shut. This is very easy for your child to do on his own without help from another adult. Let your child play at stopping and starting the sound while you dance and stop appropriately – eventually he'll be aware that his actions are affecting yours and that he is in control!

☺   *Home-made sound-matching game* – This one takes lots of effort and a few days to put together, but could become a firm favourite and a springboard to other listening games. Start with a collection of five photos of items in and around your own home, for example:

- the car
- the tap running into the bath
- the kettle
- the washing machine
- the radio.

Have two copies of each photo and stick one set onto a piece of card. The tricky part is taping each of these. If you have a Dictaphone this may be the easiest option; however, most tape players have a record facility. Make sure you record at least ten seconds of each and that you don't choose a sound that your child finds uncomfortable (for example, the vacuum cleaner). Leave a pause in the taping between sounds so that your child knows when one has stopped and the other has started. When you have completed the game by placing all the photos on their matching pairs, walk around the house and listen to the items again in real life.

☺   There are lots of talk-back toys available in gift and toy shops – the child talks to the toy and it tapes and plays back the noise. Often these are in the form of parrot toys, but other versions are coming into the market. Your child can make any sort of sound or speech attempts and hear how his own voice sounds, or you can make simple sounds (such as vowel sounds) and encourage him to copy. Often listening to speech through electronic toys (provided the pitch and volume are not uncomfortable) is less confrontational and anxiety-inducing than attending to the additional social demands (such as eye contact) that come with human interaction. Electronic learning devices are, however, only a supplementary aid to encourage purposeful noises and speech.

Remember that the process of playing and communicating with your child should be an enjoyable process for you *both*. If you really immerse yourself in the enjoyment of the activity for its own sake (rather than what you feel your child will accomplish), if you laugh and smile and relish the processes involved, then your child too will begin to understand that simply being with you is good and that his behaviours and interactions (*all* of them) are important.

Auditory Integration Training

For parents who haven't heard of AIT, it is worth mentioning. Many parents have reported good results with this therapy as a means to helping children with auditory processing problems. AIT was originated by Dr Guy Berard, a surgeon who was interested in how the muscles and nerves in the ear worked with the brain and balance organs as a complete process. When messages from systems in the ear are not being processed by the brain as they should, then individuals become hypersensitive to certain frequencies and also have problems modulating the sounds of their own voices. AIT uses modulated music to train ear muscle reflexes and increase the brain's ability to filter incoming sound. No one really knows the specific science behind why this works; however, the therapy has been around for a number of years now and appears to have helped many individuals. As with any therapy, be sensible; if your child doesn't seem comfortable – stop.

For further details on AIT see the references at the back of the book. A research summary data sheet is available from The Listen to Learn Centre, Precise Communication, Milton House, 532 City Road, Edgbaston, Birmingham B17 8LN, United Kingdom.

Chapter 7

Turn-Taking In Play

Theory of mind and social development.

The term 'theory of mind' refers to the ability to understand or 'mind-read' the thoughts, feelings and beliefs of others from what they communicate to us – not just through language but through voice tone, facial expression, body language etc.

We also have other social devices that help the smooth-running of our interactions and give the listener extra clues about our intended meaning: we tell white lies to save people's feelings; we have an awareness of their 'social space' and are careful not to move into it; we make allowances for mistakes and misunderstandings in the hope that others will do the same for us. We are also aware of how much others know about the background to a particular topic of conversation and fill in what they might need to know as we go along. We 'turn-take' in conversation by giving out and reading subtle clues for when the speaker has finished and it is our turn.

Even though we might consciously reflect on how what we say or do may make someone feel or why they have behaved in a certain way, much of our social experience 'just happens' as if some subconscious mechanism is constantly guiding our brain to oversee this sophisticated and complicated process of social inter-action.

In children this social communication ability develops from a very early age. For example:

> Two-year-old Max pretends that his teddy is alive. He watches as Mummy collaborates in the activity, making teddy talk and move, yet he 'knows that she knows' that teddy isn't really alive, but colludes with the pretense because it is fun.

> Five-year-old Jenny who has autism watches Mummy play the same game and looks confused. She takes the bear and repeatedly lies it flat on the floor.
>
> 'Look, Jenny – he's alive' says Mum. Jenny (who is very able and verbal) replies, 'He's a toy' and stops the game again.
>
> Jenny doesn't understand that her Mum *wants* to play the teddy game and her problems with imaginative thought mean she doesn't know for *sure* that Mum already knows the bear isn't really alive.

Children with autism are often thought to have 'mind-blindness' because even if they have sufficient language skills they still find understanding the thoughts, feelings and beliefs of others diffi-cult.

Why is turn-taking difficult for children on the autism spectrum?

The ability to turn-take relies on this same process that allows us to mind-read.

In order to turn-take we need to:

- be aware that the other person is part of the game

- be aware that they are integral to the game – that the game would not be a game without them

- judge when it is our turn and be patient when it is the other's turn

- be aware of what they are doing – in some games this affects what our next move will be

- try ultimately to predict what they are thinking and what they might do next so that we can adjust our actions in order to win a game

- and at its most sophisticated we may bluff, double bluff or deliberately give out false nonverbal signals to confuse the other player.

Given that a lack of social understanding underpins the autistic condition, for children on the autism spectrum, all forms of social 'turn-taking' are problematic. Structured play activities that aim to encourage the ability to turn-take from as young an age as possible not only aid learning but address the 'social' deficit that spills into so many areas of everyday living.

Awareness of others – practical activities to help

Before children with autism can attempt to understand the thoughts, intentions and feelings of others they first need to be aware that 'others' actually exist and that their physical presence and experiences are different to their own. Try the following activities to encourage this awareness:

☺ When you are holding your child, lift him to face level and point at yourself and then at him saying 'Mummy – Jacob'

☺ Whenever there are a few people in the room, ask your child to point to whoever you name – guide and prompt where necessary. You can move the game along by saying, for example, 'Point to Sue's feet/jumper/hair' etc.

☺   Have a full length mirror available for your child to look at. Stand side by side and talk about how you are different: 'Mummy is tall and Cathy is small' etc. Encourage your child to point to parts of her body whilst looking in the mirror, for example 'Point to Cathy's feet…point to Mummy's feet' etc. This is a good activity to try after a bath, as children often like to look at themselves without clothes on or with wet hair.

☺   Be brave and let your child use face paints on you (the crayon style variety would be the easiest). Sit in front of the mirror and prompt him to 'paint Mummy's nose red' etc. Have a look at the results together and then see if your child will allow you to paint *his* face.

☺   Swap clothes – put *your* jumper on your child and let him look at himself in the mirror. Try putting his socks on! Make him laugh by saying, 'These socks are too small! Look they make me fall over! Who do they belong to?… Does Jacob have small feet?'

☺   Make up a photo album of pictures of yourself as a baby or of his brothers and sisters when they were babies and also make up one of your child. Look through them and talk about when *he* was a baby and when *you* were a baby. Look at his baby clothes and toys and re-visit old camcorder footage if you have any.

☺   Throughout the day ask your child to take things to other people and physically guide him if necessary, for example 'James take the letter to Daddy'. Hold your child's hand around the letter and take him to Daddy – use lots of encouragement/re-inforcers as you feel appropriate.

☺ Enroll the help of friends and siblings and sit in a circle. Sit behind your child so that you can prompt him to remain seated. Roll a ball randomly to people in the ring and announce the name of the person you are rolling it to. They in turn roll it to someone else and announce their name. When it comes to your child encourage him to say the name of someone in the circle or point to someone for you to name. Encourage him to roll the ball – at first you may need to hold his hands around the ball and physically help him to roll it. As your child becomes more able at this activity, try moving it on as follows:

Sit your child in a 'ring' with two other adults (probably Mum and Dad), roll a ball between the three of you and whoever catches the ball must say something about themselves. Start off simply with physical descriptions, for example 'I have short hair', 'I have a red jumper on', 'My name is…' etc. Your child will need lots of support to understand the game. Have one of the adults be your child's 'voice', if necessary and touch whatever they are describing. After a few sessions try adding siblings or family friends.

Awareness of others' thoughts: practical activities to help

☺ Throughout the day keep telling your child how things make you feel. For example, if he sits on your knee, say, 'When Tom sits on Mummy's knee it makes me feel happy' or if the weather's fine, say, 'I like the sunshine – it makes me feel happy'. Only introduce 'happy' and 'sad' to start with and then add emotions such as 'worried' or 'angry'. Don't forget to attribute words to describe *his* feelings too, so that he can relate the label to the feeling, for example, 'Tom is angry…let's stamp together…'. Don't just concentrate on strong feelings, remember to tell your child when he is calm or sleepy. He won't understand the words 'calm down' unless he can remember what the feeling of calm was at the time when you labelled it for him. Understanding his own emotions is integral to his ability to understand others.

The following activities can be done as part of your structured learning activities session (see Chapter 3):

☺   Make two sets of the drawings conveying emotions shown in Chapter 12 (Being Creative – Art and Craft) and play a matching game. Place one set down on the table in front of your child and hold up the second set one at a time, saying, 'Can you find the same?' When your child correctly matches the emotion, say, 'Well done – they both feel sad'. Adjust the tone of your voice to match the expression. Use different ways to add motivation and interest to the game – for example, turn it into a posting game, or add 'hook and loop' strips to make matching a definite process. See Chapter 5 for different ideas on how to introduce this type of table-top learning. If your child is having difficulty recognizing emotions from drawings, use a set of photo cards of emotions (see the back of the book for references). Remember, this is a complex activity – judge whether your child is ready for this task. If not, leave it for a few months and concentrate on activities that increase his awareness of others.

☺   If your child consistently recognizes emotions from drawings, try matching the pictures to situations. Find a few scenarios in books, such as someone falling over, eating an ice cream, walking through the woods etc. If your child is distracted by the book then make a photocopy – you might even want to blank out the expression on the face so you can add one with a pencil while you talk. Put the 'scenario' picture in front of your child and describe simply and slowly what is happening. Ask him to match one of the emotion drawings to how the character may be feeling. Point to each emotion drawing in turn and label the feeling, for example, 'Happy, sad, cross, afraid'. Encourage your child to point to or label the appropriate feeling. Be consistent with your labels – if you choose the label 'afraid', leave the label 'worried' until later, when you think your child might understand the subtle difference; likewise choose 'angry' *or* 'cross'. For older, able children, ask them to draw an expression on the face. Always be mindful of any specific unusual fears your child may have when you do this task, you cannot expect him to say that a specific character will be happy watching the circus if your child is personally terrified of clowns. Avoid showing him images that may make him anxious, otherwise he'll lose the motivation to complete the activity. For lots of activities similar to this, try *Teaching Children with Autism to Mind-Read* by Patricia Howlin, Simon Baron-Cohen and Julie Hadwin (see the back of the book for details).

☺   If your child is coping well with this type of activity and has good language skills, invest in a set of 'Why/Because' cards (see the back of the book for the supplier). These come in pairs and show a particular scenario and its consequences, for example, 'Little girl crying because she's broken a vase etc.' Use the cards in your structured learning sessions (see Chapter 3, 'Structured Play'). Hold the card up to your child and describe what's happening, for example, 'Look, the baby's crying… why might he be crying? Does he want his Mummy? Has he broken his toy?' etc. Finally hold up the second card and describe the real reason why, 'Look he was hungry. He's eating his tea now…how does he feel?' When you are using lots of language in this way, always give your child plenty of time to answer and only expect him to concentrate in very short bursts.

☺   Use glove puppets and soft toys to demonstrate feelings. Glove puppets that squeak or make noises have good 'attention-grabbing' qualities and can be operated to express emotions through their squeaks (fast, excited squeaking, slow, sad etc.) At my home, we permanently have a particular glove puppet available throughout the day. Sometimes our son will bring it to us to play but often we use it to 'bring him back', if he's just running up and down. He'll often listen to 'Sammy Shark' rather than what we have to say! If he hits or bites or strokes the puppet we can make it react appropriately. Puppets can animate an idea in a way that appeals to all children, including those on the autism spectrum. Particularly for children with autism, puppets remove the anxiety of 'direct' interaction with another person and allow you to connect with your child through a 'third' party. Choose carefully – puppets that look like people can be a bit off-putting. Initially perhaps try an animal that you think might appeal.

☺   Throughout the day, if your child requests things, tell him what *you* want too. 'Mummy's hungry too – I want a banana.' Tell him if there are things you don't like – he might find an exaggerated response funny. Be careful not to teach him to dislike things you don't like in the process, though!

Small beginnings – turn-taking with an adult

There are many activities in all the chapters of this book that have a 'turn-taking' element to them. As well as these, try the following activities that specifically work on encouraging a child to turn-take. Work in short bursts with lots of motivating reinforcers. This level of direction and intervention can be uncomfortable to a child with autism who is putting most of his energy into 'cutting off'. If he continues to resist, try being indirect – play with a sibling, a teddy, or even make a video of you 'turn-taking' (see Chapter 11).

☺   Ball runs or (marble runs for older children) have a good potential as a rewarding activity that can be done as a turn taking exercise. There are lots of versions on the market. Also try products such as "pound a ball" (see the back of the book for toy suppliers). Split the balls between the two of you (just two each to begin with). Announce whose turn it is and encourage your child to wait for his turn (this is a good activity to also try with a sibling – with you supporting the child with autism). Use 'ready…steady…go' or '1…2…3…wheeeee!'. Make sure you praise your child specifically for waiting (saying 'good…waiting') rather than general non-specific praise. Encourage him to pay attention to whoever's turn it is and to join in saying 'ready…steady…go' etc.

☺ You can turn-take putting pieces into puzzles, putting shapes into shape sorters, posting pictures into a home-made post box, cutting shapes out of play dough, jumping off steps – in fact anything you can get your child interested and motivated in can be moved on and turned into a turn-taking exercise. Be creative – use your own participation as a way to introduce a new idea into the game for your child to imitate.

☺ Play an 'I can see' or 'pointing' game – look out of the window and take turns to say, 'I can see a…bird' etc., or simply support your child to point at something in the garden saying, 'Tom can see a tree…Mummy can see an aeroplane.'

☺ 'Make a Scene' cards are easily available. They consist of a fold-out cardboard scene and reusable 'peel and stick' stickers. Choose one that you feel has special appeal for your child. Lay open the scene in front of the two of you and have the sheet of stickers at the side – don't use the full sheet, just six to start with (three each). Take turns at choosing a sticker and placing it on the scene. You may need another adult to support your child and to keep the activity on track as a turn-taking exercise (rather than the two of you simply making a scene together). Announce what you will be putting on the scene, for example, 'Mummy's putting a duck in the pond…now it's

Lucy's turn'. Keep the activity fun and motivating; make the stickers 'do' things to make your child laugh, or make a teddy be the third 'turn-taker'. The activity may be about encouraging your child to turn-take, but remember it's also about playing.

☺   For a child that finds the sticker scenes too fiddly and frustrating to handle, try making a 'scene' game yourself, tailoring it exactly to what appeals to your child. You will need some strong card, pieces of different coloured felt, scissors, glue and 'peel and stick' hook and loop tape.

Decide on a 'scene' – you might try the seaside (after a trip) or you might choose something obscure like a cupboard with shelves (this appealed to my son's 'container' interest). Cover a piece of A4-size card with a piece of felt for the background colour – if you're doing an outdoor scene, split it into green/blue or, for the seaside, yellow/blue. For the cupboard 'scene', make a simple oblong shape and a door and put strips of black felt in as shelves. Then make a collection of six to eight items that you can put into the cupboard, 'turn-taking' style. They can be as simple or intricate as you like – a teddy, a ball, a car, a drum, etc. Simply cover pieces of card with the felt, draw the shape on the reverse and then cut it out. Finally put pieces of hook and loop on the reverse and onto the 'scene' card so that they can be stuck onto the scene.

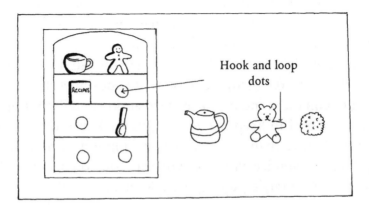

Hook and loop dots

You can then use the activity in the same way as the sticker scenes. You could even take this one step further and make two identical scenes and play a 'screen' game similar to the listening game detailed in Chapter 6. Set up a partition between yourself and your child in the middle of the table (see illustration in Chapter 6) – a second adult may have to support your child in following your instructions, for example, 'Jack put the ball in the cupboard' etc. If your child is verbal, aim for him to tell *you* where to put an item, or, if nonverbal the second adult could encourage him to point at the item he chooses and the adult can then call out the instruction. Make your child aware that what you do is contingent on *his* instruction.

Turn-taking with peers and siblings

It's not always possible (or fair) for siblings to be pulled into all activities with their brother or sister. However, whenever an activity is simple and fun enough for the child with autism to play at a level that doesn't hamper the enjoyment of the others, then it should be encouraged. Chapter 9 ('Physical Games and Activities') in particular has lots of ideas that can be adapted to turn-taking with siblings. Other children provide role models that simply cannot be reproduced by an adult and it is vital that children with autism have access to being included in 'normal' play with their peers and siblings.

If brothers and sisters are old enough to have their sibling's problem explained in terms they can understand, then let them have that information. There are some excellent books around that deal exactly with this topic (see the back of the book for details).

Structured turn-taking away from physical activities takes a little more effort and requires more adult intervention and direction. Try the following:

☺   Sit the children in a circle. (You may wish to support the child with autism at first but aim to move away a little so that he's playing independently as part of the group.) Encourage the children to pass a drum around the circle whilst you sing:

(To the tune of 'London Bridge is falling down')

Pass the drum around the ring,
round the ring,
round the ring,
pass the drum around the ring,
till it gets to…Stephen.

Stephen then bangs the drum whilst the others sing (to the same tune).

Bang the drum
Bang, bang, bang
Bang, bang, bang
Bang, bang, bang
Bang the drum
bang, bang bang
Bang bang bang bang bang.

Of course you can change the game by changing the instrument – try maraccas/shakers, blowers, bells etc.

To keep your child focused on sitting, let him have a special cushion or chair. You might even want to create a picture prompt for 'sitting' that you can place at the side of him, or that you can hold up to remind him to stay sitting.

☺   On a similar theme you could 'pass a bag around the ring' using a bag of 'themed' articles – plastic animals, colour-themed objects, toy food items etc. When the bag 'lands on' a child, he removes an object and says what it is. For a nonverbal child you might want to create a set of pictures mounted on a card. When your child removes an object, he then points to the matching picture on the card (don't forget to write the name of the object under the picture so that he can create an association between the picture and the words). Remind the other children in the game to give your child plenty of time, and encourage them not to shout out the answer.

Aids to help turn-taking

- Try letting the child/adult whose turn it is wear a hat or badge – this gives the child with autism a physical and visual clue for when it is both his turn and others'.

- Provide a special area that your child must remain in/on – this could be a carpet tile, a cushion or a small chair.

- Use a visual timer (see the back of the book for suppliers) or a simple cooking timer (if your child doesn't mind the bell) so that he is aware of how long the activity will take.

- Build the 'turn-taking' activity into his picture diary (use picture references at the back of the book) and/or use a reinforcer (a rewarding activity, treat, or special interest) that he can do afterwards to motivate him to partake.

- Wherever possible, introduce special interest toys, pictures and ideas.

Turn-taking in everyday life

- Try to seize on moments throughout the day. Try to introduce 'turn-taking' and awareness of others through routine activities. for example:

'Anna wants juice…Mummy wants coffee.'
'Anna sits down…Mummy sits down.'

'Anna brushes hair…Mummy brushes hair.'

- In your structured learning sessions, take some turns yourself at whatever activity you are doing, for example, matching, sorting, posting.

- If your child is engaged in a solitary activity such as spinning, vocalizing, stacking, take a turn yourself and announce 'Mummy's turn'. Be careful not to just take whatever your child might be playing with – use your own version. Copy your child's action and then wait for him to do it again. Try to tune into the activity as a turn-taking exercise.

It's easy to revolve your family around the needs of a special child without pointing out to him that other people have their own needs, feelings, desires. Tell your child when you or others in the family are hungry, thirsty, hot, cold, sleepy etc. Not only does this model appropriate verbal labels for these attributes, but it serves as a reminder to him that there are other feelings in the room as well as his own.

Keep your language stripped down to the essentials and be aware that even though you are attributing a label to his feelings, his experience of the world is very different to your own. You can only make a guess at what is truly going on!

Chapter 8

Physical Games and Activities

Sensory integration problems

What causes children with autism to have problems with balance and co-ordination, to be hyperactive or under-active and to be distressed by certain movements and textures?

When my son was causing us concern at around eighteen months, one of the most prominent difficulties he had was poor balance and co-ordination. Even beyond his diagnosis at two and a half, he was falling and banging into things at an alarming rate. After we had ruled out physical problems with his hips, legs, vision and hearing it became plain that the processing problems that were part of his autism also encompassed his 'abnormal' clumsiness. In a quest to understand why this was and what activities might help, I came across the work of Dr Jean Ayres[1] and the theory of *sensory integration*. The sensory processing problems she described were the first and most common-sense explanation of the physical problems and odd behaviours that accompanied his autistic symptoms.

All children on the autism spectrum have sensory-processing difficulties to varying degrees. The sensory problems mentioned most often in this book are auditory processing problems; these are the ones most parents are quick to recognise. Their child might react extremely to certain noises, covering his ears or screaming, or may hold articles that make noises very close to his ears in an unusual way. Children with autism may also have sensory processing difficulties in the areas of taste, smell, touch and vision, resulting in rigid diets, resistance to being held or cuddled, over-sensitivities to certain clothing textures, bright sunshine or vivid colours and a whole host of other confusing behaviours. Not all children display all these sensitivities, but often troublesome behaviours can be related to a sensory processing problem.

Why include such detail on sensory processing in a chapter on physical games and activities?

Another form of sensory processing is the means by which information from our eyes tells our brains where our heads and bodies physically are in the space they occupy – not just whether we are upright or lying down but the varying degrees and movements in between. This is called the *vestibular system*. Problems with processing vestibular information are not so obvious as sound sensitivities, but all children with autism can benefit from playing physical games and activities that help to exercise the brain's ability to process this type of information. Non-autistic children naturally refine this ability through energetic physical playing that involves kicking throwing, balancing, jumping etc.

Children with autism who have problems processing vestibular information may display all or some of the following behaviours:

- Aversion to being lifted off the ground or tilted.
- Throwing their head back without any sense of what may be behind it.
- Problems correcting balance and frequent falling, banging into things.

- Problems manoeuvering around obstacles on the floor.

- Being particularly rough when playing – not knowing how to adjust touch so that it is not painful!

- Hyperactivity or unusually low levels of activity.

- Rocking/head-banging.

The above is by no means a definitive list.

Sensory integration therapy is a specific skilled therapy that must only be conducted by a trained and experienced professional. However, as parents, it helps to know what obstacles are stopping our children from experiencing and exploring the world in the same way as their non-autistic peers, as often these are not always obvious. By always being aware and observant of sensory processing problems we can attempt to coax our children into the world of physical play in a gentle and understanding manner that doesn't thrust upon them sensations that are physically and emotionally distressing. At the same time we can introduce play activities that encourage the developing brain to work more effectively at processing sensory input and vestibular information. Physical play activities are therefore vital for the healthy development not just of the body but of the brain.

Getting started

As with all the play suggestions in this book, try to find a way to communicate to your child what is going to happen and include physical games as part of your child's structured play activities – see Chapter 3 ('Structured Play') for suggestions on how to do this. Never force your child to participate in a physical activity that he clearly is not enjoying or encourage him to do an activity beyond his physical ability. Remember that in your physical play with your child, he needs to be aware that *you* are a vital part of the activity – i.e. that you are giving the activity *joint attention*; that the activity needs the two of you to work together to make it happen. Therefore, if you suddenly find yourself sitting alongside your child doing nothing while he repeatedly throws a ball against the wall, then somehow the game has gone off focus! In finding this, don't panic. He needs some time to explore the activity himself, but after sufficient time, try to redirect his solitary play back to a joint activity.

The use of *rhymes* associated with these games helps your child in the following way:

- Increases his understanding about what you are actually doing.

- Draws his attention to *your* involvement.

- Encourages and draws his attention to the activity.

- Helps his language by using the same repetitive, familiar and rhythmic verses for him to anticipate and imitate.

- Helps him to judge when to throw/catch/roll by synchronizing rhymes to his physical movements.

- Makes him aware of his own physical movements and that he can deliberately time and co-ordinate his actions with a rhyme to increase his own enjoyment.

- Creates opportunities for him to communicate by building up anticipation to create the motivation to attempt to communicate during any pauses you leave for him. For example, once he is familiar with a rhyme, leave pauses for him to finish the rhyme and anticipate what will happen next (i.e. a throw in the air, or a jump or a tickle).

For more detail on why rhythm and rhymes are useful for children with autism see Chapter 6 (Music). Remember to encourage siblings to join in wherever possible.

With all physical activities, take some sensible safety precautions – clear the room of any clutter and obstacles that your child may fall on. Scatter cushions close by or, better still, invest in a padded exercise mat (especially if you are not playing on carpeted floor).

Ball games

☺   The outsize inflatable ball – these types of balls are frequently available from high street shops. If you have difficulty try one of the special needs suppliers (details at the back of the book).

Accustom your child gently to the feel of the ball first by patting and rolling it around the room.

Stand your child on the ball facing you whilst you sit on a chair/sofa supporting the ball between your knees (if there is another adult in the room, get him/her to hold the ball). Hold your child securely under the arms (in case the ball rolls away from under his feet) and gently bounce him up and down. Help your child anticipate when the bouncing will start by saying 'ready...steady...go'. Follow your child's reactions – he might want to keep going forever or he might only want one or two bounces. If your child finds standing face to face uncomfortable then stand him with his back to you. Work at getting your child to finish your 'ready...steady...' sentence. Try bouncing him to the following rhyme:

Bouncing Peter one, two, three
Like a frog, can you see?
Ribbit ribbit ribbit...wheeee!

(At this point lift your child off the ball into the air. Try to get your child to finish the rhyme with a 'Wheeee!')

☺   Lying your child tummy down on the ball while you gently rock it will help his balance and can often be a slight pressure sensation that children with autism enjoy. Remember, if your child objects it may not simply be because he is frightened he will fall (the natural assumption); it could be that his vestibular processing difficulty is such that he feels disorientated with his feet off the floor. If this is the case, don't abandon the activity altogether but leave it for a month and try again at monthly intervals. If he enjoys it, try to encourage him to stretch out on the ball and balance – with you only lightly stabilizing it. Capitalize on the communication potential of the activity by pretending to wobble the ball and saying, 'Will he fall…? Yes?' Wait for a communicative gesture to indicate 'more' before returning your child to the ball and the activity.

Small ball play

Work with a selection of balls of different textures (remember that too much brightly coloured patterning may be distracting). Start with a medium-size soft ball that is easy to grasp.

☺   Try sitting opposite your child and rolling the ball to him. If he is not ready to roll it back to you, have another adult sit next to or behind him to show him what to do. If you feel your child is uncomfortable sitting facing you, try sitting alongside him and bouncing the ball to him off the skirting board. Again use the opportunity to increase his awareness of language by singing rhymes or just commentating on what you are doing in very simple repetitive language. Try the following rhymes substituting your child's name, ball colour etc.

This is a ball, soft and round
Rolling, rolling on the ground
Rolling to...Katy, roll back to me
Back to Katy, one, two,...three!

or

Mummy rolls the red ball,
Bounces off the white wall
Ready, steady, go into...Katy's hands
Katy rolls the red ball
Bounces off the white wall
Ready, steady, go into...Mummy's hands!

Remember to pause for your child to fill in the rhyme.

If your child is showing no interest in this game try the same activity but using a toy car, pushing it to each other — with a few word substitutions in the rhymes.

☺   Set a large box in the centre of the room. Have a ball each and take turns throwing it into the box. To develop the game after a few sessions, reduce the size of the box and the ball. After a while, try removing one ball so that your child has to wait for his turn.

Throwing throwing throwing, one, two...three
Into the big box – Jonathon and me
Mum's turn first – ready, steady...throw
Jonathon now – ready...steady...go!

or

Are we ready? Let's get steady
Taking turns to throw
Jack goes first, then Mummy next
Ready...steady...go!

Alternate sizes and textures of balls (include squeaky soft balls, and those with bells/rattles inside). This can also be played with bean bags and soft toys.

Large hoop

A large plastic hoop can help children with autism understand spatial terms such as 'through', 'in', 'out', 'over'. It can also help them understand how their body fits inside a physical boundary. Try the following:

☺   Take turns jumping in and out of a hoop on the floor. To make it easier for your child to see where the hoop is on a patterned carpet, place it on a plain rug/mat. Jumping with two feet is quite a physical achievement, so encourage any kind of movement from stepping to hurling his whole body in.

> Mummy jumps, now *I'm...in*
> Standing in the ring.
> James jumps, now *he's...in*
> Standing in the ring.
>
> Mummy jumps, now *I'm...out*
> Outside the ring.
> James jumps, now *he's...out*
> Both out of the ring.
>
> Together jump, now *we're...in*
> Inside the ring.
> Together jump, now *we're...out*
> Outside the ring.

Don't forget to emphasise the words 'I'm in' etc. and to pause to allow your child to finish the rhyme with the words 'in' and 'out'
    or

Jump *in* and clap 1, 2, 3
Jump *out* and clap 1, 2, 3
Walk *round* the ring
And follow me!

Later you might add variation with 'Hop in and clap 1, 2, 3',
'Step in…' etc.

Indoor ball pit

Children with autism can find indoor soft-play areas stressful. Lots
of activity from other children, unpredictable and high noise
levels and unfamiliar environments may mean that you have
decided that your child doesn't like this type of play when in fact it
may be a multitude of other factors that are putting him off. There
are ways to create mini soft-play activities in the home, where your
child can benefit greatly from stretching his co-ordination ability
and balance. You may find he loves the challenge of an activity that
doesn't force language or imagination on him. If so, try some
pre-planned outings to soft-play areas at specifically quiet times
(try ringing in advance).

☺   Try filling a small paddling pool or shallow box with
plastic balls (available in packs of 100/200 etc. from many toy
stores). Let your child explore the pit at his own pace – it may
feel unnerving at first to be on such an unstable surface. If he is
very unsure, try getting teddy to play first – make him dive into
the balls, bury him, make him pop up again – this is a good
game in it's own right! It may be worth burying wrapped
biscuits/sweets/favourite objects to coax your child in.
Alternatively get in yourself and let him sit between your legs.
Maybe just look at a book or listen to music if he's still unsure.

Once he's in the pit, try some activities to encourage him to take direction from you and engage in interactions wherever possible (all the time he will be getting used to the sensation of the balls):

☺   Sink a bucket in the centre (with the rim above the surface of the balls) and take turns throwing in balls. You might want to try teaching colours by choosing only one colour at a time.

You could use this rhyme:

> Red red red – this is a red ball (holding it up)
> Throw throw throw, 1, 2,...3
> Red balls in the bucket, red balls in my hands
> First goes...(point to your child) Stephen and then it's me!

☺   Try burying your child slowly ball by ball – count out the balls as you place them on him. Prompt him to *wait* until you say 'ready...steady...go!' and he can pop up out of the balls and surprise you. This takes some concentrated effort to wait for your command, so try just a few balls at first and gradually make him wait longer.

☺   Experiment with the feel of the balls. Try removing socks, or putting gloves on an older child and then getting him to pick up a ball. This helps him to discriminate between the feel of different surfaces and how his body relates to them. On this same theme you could try replacing the balls altogether with a different texture; fill the pool with polystyrene chips (put a large sheet under it first to help with the tidy up!), crumpled paper (a torn-up old roll of wallpaper is cleaner than newsprint), or spread out a large piece of fur fabric inside the pool. Try with socks first and then without to highlight the contrast in feel.

Large boxes

All children love playing in large empty cardboard boxes and by and large this includes children with autism too. They may need help imagining that the same box can be anything from a train to a house to a boat, but the feel and novelty can be still quite tempting. Before you start cutting windows and doors and drawing wheels, let your child simply play with the box as it is. Explore the limitations of its size, observe whether he feels fearful at the prospect of going inside and work on demonstrating that this is a fun activity.

☺   Try removing the top and bottom so that in effect you have a cardboard tunnel for him to crawl through. Progress to tipping a box on its side for him to crawl into. Fill the box with cushions and favourite objects. Boxes of all shapes and sizes have great 'peek-a-boo' potential.

Making a tactile box

☺   Attach lengths of ribbon to the open side of a box lying on its side so your child has to crawl through the ribbon to get inside. You could try putting a length of 'hook and loop' tape (the peel-and-stick variety) to the top of the box and attach the ribbon to the other piece of 'hook and loop'. You can then make additional lengths with different objects.

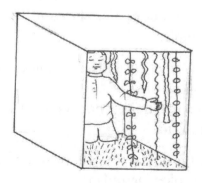

Objects you might like to try:

- cotton reels threaded onto string
- old CDs that catch the light as they spin
- beads
- bells
- shells
- Cheerios or Wheetos (if your child is NOT on a GF diet!).

Ransack the house for bits and pieces and observe which appeals most to your child.

For safety reasons be careful about the size of objects you use for very young children or those that are likely to put the objects in their mouth.

☺   Try lining the four sides of the box with different fabrics, for example, felt, fur, silk, hessian.

Imaginative uses for boxes

☺   When your child is happy being in and around the boxes then you can play *imaginatively*. To help your child's imagination, find a picture of what the box is going to be (house, boat, train etc.) and prop it up close by saying 'a boat like the one in the book'. Use the same dialogue with each activity, for example:

> 'Thomas is in a boat. Here comes a big wave – it's rocking the boat.'
> 'Jack is in the train; choo choo it's stopping at the station…etc.'

Once again use the box as something *your* child can relate to – car, bus, shop, cooker, aeroplane.

As with all your playing be sure your child understands the concept of what the box is representing, pretending the box is an aeroplane is only useful if he is familiarized with the word and what it is. This is one type of play where video modeling could be very useful, either film yourself or a sibling/s playing appropriately and using appropriate language in a very simple play scenario; for further ideas on using video see Chapter 11 ('Television Potential')

Human jack-in-the-box

☺   'Peek-a-boo' type games are great for encouraging children with autism to participate *jointly*. Take it in turns to hide inside the box and pop up again.

Try the following rhyme.

> (When it's your child's turn, replace 'Mummy' with his name.)
> Where is Mummy, where can she be?
> Is she hiding, where is she?
> Are you waiting? Quietly
> Ready, steady 1, 2,…3!

or

> The big dark box was quiet and still
> What do you think is inside?
> Is it a bear, or a dog, or a bunny?
> It's none of those…it's Mummy!

Puppet theatre

This is a grand name for a simple box-screen to hide *you* using a glove puppet. Start with one character (a familiar animal), or use a simple silhouette shape on a stick. Enlist the help of a second adult to draw your child's attention to what's going on, by asking questions (and providing the answers if necessary) about what your child can see. Try to enact something your child has done recently. Siblings may like to get involved in this one by doing the puppet show for you.

Trampoline

Many parents have reported that the trampoline is an essential piece of equipment and helps prolong the life of furniture! It can readily provide the sensations that some children seem to crave and can also be used as a piece of play equipment to encourage interaction. Many parents of older children move on to a large outdoor trampoline in the garden, but for children up to six years the small trampoline with a holding bar is fine. For lots of ideas on how to encourage interaction on the trampoline try Chapter 9. ('Outdoor Play').

Indoor slide and balance beam

One of the most useful pieces of indoor physical play equipment we have at home is a plank of wood that is approximately 1.5 metres long and wide enough to walk down easily. I sanded all the edges smooth and painted it with my son's favourite *Winnie the Pooh* character. On the reverse side I painted 'footprints' for where to place his feet. You could do something very simple like painted circles or ovals depending on how much time you have.

Try the following, but remember to always supervise your child, even when he can play competently on the beam.

☺   Introduce the beam first by placing it flat on the ground and playing 'follow the leader' along its length. Try putting something your child wants at the end, for him to retrieve.

Later try propping it about 10 cm off the floor – use blocks of wood or bricks.

Once he is confident with it, place one end on a sofa to make a slide – there are lots of crawling under, crawling up, sliding down possibilities.

☺   If your child is really enjoying this type of activity and can take some direction, try making a 'circuit' for him, for example, 'across the beam, jump into the hoop, lift it over your head, ten jumps on the trampoline and a big jump onto a pile of cushions!'. Remember to introduce each element first on its own, otherwise a collection of challenges could be completely baffling.

Cushions

Floor cushions and squashy bean bags are good for taking the strain off your furniture! They can also be used as part of your physical indoor games sessions. Try the following:

☺   With a little double-sided tape or masking tape, stick a large simple picture (cut them from magazines or do a very simple line drawing) to each of three or four cushions. Place the cushions at the other end of the room and play a 'ready…steady…go' game where your child has to fetch you the cushion that you request (according to the picture). Once he is doing this easily, add some variety by asking for 'something I can eat' (your child brings the cushion with picture of the apple on), or 'something furry' (he brings the picture of the cat). If he doesn't want to fetch the cushion, ask him to *jump* on the appropriate cushion or even return it by holding it in his teeth (especially if you have a child that craves the oral stimulation he gets from biting!). As well as pictures, you might try letters, numbers and words. For children developing literacy skills, try putting a different word on each cushion and making simple three word sentences.

☺   Cushions can also be used for stepping stones and easy to catch throwing games.

☺   Some children with autism simply love having cushions thrown (gently) at them, or being made into a 'cushion sandwich', with you applying gentle pressure. Once again you can build in lots of pauses to build up anticipation and create an opportunity for your child to communicate.

Skittles

☺   A set of skittles (a good size that are easy to stand up) are useful for turn taking and 'ready…steady…go' type games. Also try singing a version of 'ten green bottles' – stand four or five skittles in a line and sing:

> Four happy skittles standing in a row
> Four happy skittles standing in a row
> And if one happy skittle should decide to go [remove the
>   skittle out of sight as if it's running!]
> There'll be three happy skittles standing in a row.

☺   Don't forget skittles can also be used for other number work – write the numbers one to three (to start with) on separate large sheets of paper and encourage your child to set up the correct number of skittles on each sheet. As a reward for completing the task he can knock them over.

Other useful physical play toys

☺   *Bouncy castles* – These are becoming quite readily available for home/garden use and can be a satisfying activity for energetic children.

☺   *Children's plastic golf set* – In the sense that it is not a team game as such, golf can be a sport that children with autism can develop an interest in and occasionally excel at. For very young children a simple set is easy to use and understand. Try creating a distinct target rather than aimlessly hitting the ball – a large cardboard box on its side with an arch shaped hole cut out is ideal.

☺   Small hoops or frisbees (the hollow disc type) are useful for hoopla (using pop bottles filled with sand/water) or for stepping games.

☺   *Bean bags/frogs* – These can be used in a turn-taking game, throwing them into containers, or used to help your child's listening and language comprehension skills as follows:

Set up a bucket and a box in front of your child and give him a bean bag. Ask him to, 'Throw the bean bag into the box'. He has to listen to and remember which container he has to aim for. Start with just two elements (bucket and box) and one bean bag. As he consistently gets this right, add more bean bags and a third element (a jug). As your child gets better at this task he might manage to listen to something like, 'Throw the yellow beanbag into the large box' (choice of small, medium and large). Ask your speech and language therapist about further activities you can try to increase your child's receptive language skills.

☺   *Balloons* – Bat them to each other with homemade bats made from stiff cardboard (or make any shape to use as a bat hands, feet, etc.). Draw or stick a picture your child may be responsive to onto the surface. (This need only be something simple like a picture of an ice-cream or may be a particular interest like a crane. You might also try a photo of a pet, car or house). Look out for a helicopter-type balloon whereby the balloon sends a propeller whizzing round the room – a great attention-grabber! Blow them up, pause and wait for your child to indicate for you to let go.

☺   *Funky Foot Mat / Funky Piano* – See references at the back of the book for where to find this type of toy. It is basically a mat that responds with a sound when you put your feet on the footprints on its surface. It either comes in the form of a keyboard or has shapes and colours that respond with sounds. Try walking with your child standing on your feet, holding on round your legs.

You could ask your child to stand on a particular colour and see if he will ask you to do the same, or hold up a coloured foot shape and say, 'Sam jump on same'. The rewarding sound from this type of toy can provide just the extra amount of motivation needed for your child to allow you to direct him.

☺   *Tents and tunnels and cubes* – These pop-up play tents are readily available, easy to store and have great potential for 'now you see me – now you don't' games. Chapter 9 ('Outdoor Play') has lots of ideas for how to use them.

I hope this chapter has fuelled you with ideas not only for the *types* of toys that might appeal to your child but how you can use them positively with a style of playing that encourages interaction and joint attention, whilst your child engages in the physical play he needs to relieve some of the stress that being on the autism spectrum constantly puts him under.

1   Dr. A. Jean Ayres originated the theory of *sensory integration,* which has since been taken up and recognized by child development clinicians and occupational therapists, who introduce specific exercises to help children integrate sensory input more effectively. If you are interested in finding out more about sensory integration therapy, the relevant addresses are at the back of this book.

Chapter 9

Outdoor Play

Problems and solutions

For children with autism, playing outside can have the potential to increase behaviours that enable them to 'cut off' from interaction. Outdoor play is often less structured, offers more choice and has many distractions. On top of this there are unexpected noises, smells, bright sunshine and masses of visual input. Things move unexpectedly – flying birds, insects and even trees swaying in the breeze.

All this extra sensory input can lead to a child being overwhelmed with too much information to process and having difficulty moving his attention from one thing to the next (he may appear deaf because he simply cannot shift his focus from the brightness of the sky to listening to your voice). In addition, he may be anxious about something particular, like the sound of a bee or the lawnmower next door. All of this can lead to tantrums, distress or withdrawn repetitive/obsessive activities before you even *start* to play.

Before you take your child outdoors stand outside yourself for a minute and check for the following:

- If it's very hot and bright make sure you have a sunshade available and hat or sunglasses for your child to wear (put these on before you go outside). If sun cream is necessary, again put this on before you go out.

- If there are loud noises from garden equipment, wait until the work is finished before you go out. Or, if he will wear them, have a pair of headphones or earmuffs ready for unexpected loud noises (aeroplanes, lawn mowers etc.)

- If your child is sensitive to smells, check there are no barbecues next door or strong 'country' smells.

- If insects are a problem, don't dress yourself or your child in yellow which will attract flying insects and if you have a particular plant that attracts bees and wasps, think about relocating it to a different part of the garden or make a note to get rid of it.

Safety

- For clumsy, unco-ordinated children, keep legs and knees covered even in hot weather (with light cotton trousers), have a red towel or flannel to hand for bumps (red disguises any spots of blood and prevents further distress) and have a first-aid kit available.

- For children that hate plasters, a length of clean cotton material used as a bandage (even for small scrapes) will hide the bumps and feel soothing.

- Remove obvious hazards such as nettles, large stones and pots that can be tripped over.

- To make steps more visible, try chalking a bright colour on each one.

- Make sure open water is made safe and water features that can be touched are filled with clean water in case it's drunk.

- For very young children, children that insist on eating stones/soil etc. or where gardens are filled with hazards, try sectioning off an area of grass as an outdoor play pen as follows:

For a movable structure try making four separate panels about 1.5 meters long, each consisting of two poles about a meter high with a pointed end that can be hammered into the grass. Across the two poles attach either waterproof fabric (like a wind break) or the natural bamboo screening that can bought on a roll from garden centres. The four panels can be hammered into the ground to form a square – you only need two or three if it's against a wall. To avoid having to construct a gate, make it short enough for you to step over (or use a small step). This safe play area can have many purposes – if your child is particularly anxious you can play in the safe area first, by which time he will be getting used to the feeling of being in the garden; for a child likely to fall it is somewhere safe to leave him if you have to answer the door etc. It can also be used as an area to bring your child back to for a structured play activity, as it removes a certain amount of distraction and helps refocus your child's attention back on you. Your child may like the feeling of somewhere enclosed to go if something unexpected happens like an aeroplane goes overhead and will learn that these things, though unpleasantly loud, are not a threat to him. If he just ran back indoors it would not help him cope when you are out and about, away from the house. Even though creating a safe den is a little time-consuming, it may be very much worth the effort and will last quite a few summers.

The benefits of outdoor play

Aside from the difficulties outlined above, if you and your child can find a way to play outdoors, the benefits are important. As well as the usual health-related benefits that outdoor play has for all children, for children with autism it:

- provides an opportunity to play with siblings and friends in physical games that are easier to understand and take part in than complex imaginative games or games with rules such as card and board games

- provides the space for hyperactive children to run off excess energy and have a better night's sleep

- provides an environment in which to experiment with messy art activities and water play

- is a good practice ground for coping with 'processing' lots of sensory input in a safe and controlled environment

- is a good environment to practice physical skills such as balancing and co-ordinating movements on different surfaces

For the child's parents, outdoor play provides an opportunity to watch and respond to the way their child reacts to the stimulation of an environment that changes all the time according to the weather, the light and the seasons. He may notice things you've never seen before or enjoy sounds, sensations and reflections that have never occurred to you. Allow some 'free time' where he does what he wants. Shadow him and imitate his actions, drag the twig across the gravel, flick water droplets off leaves, squint at the sunlight pouring through trellis – experience *his* interpretation of the outdoors as well as showing him yours, join in and be responsive. Work out what elements he finds attractive and incorporate them into your games.

The need for structure

As with all the play activities in this book, find a way to communicate to your child (with picture prompts) – first that he will be going outside and second, what specific activity he will be playing with. Don't forget to take photos of your child playing a particular game so that they can be used in the future as a picture prompt. If your garden is too small or unsuitable for some of the activities, try friends/relatives, gardens, or go to the park early, before it gets busy.

Some children will need a reward/reinforcer for attempting a particular activity. Try the activities your child will spontaneously engage in, for example, the trampoline first and then use this as a reward for something more challenging. Don't forget to communicate to your child (with a picture prompt) that this preferred activity will follow the one that is not as attractive.

Getting started – games and activities

As well as the following ideas, don't forget to check Chapters 8 and 10 for further ideas on *physical activities* and *water play* that can be used outside.

Pavement chalking

☺ Draw a circle on the floor and practice taking turns jumping into it – try the rhymes suggested in Chapter 8 ('Physical Play') for jumping in and out of a hoop.

☺ Try the Pavement Chalker by Fisher Price (see references at the end of the book). This is a wheel on a handle, with a clasp to hold the chalk. The child pushes it along the ground like a line marker used to mark out courts etc. The activity itself is easy and rewarding and you can add tasks such as joining up two dots with a straight line or making wavy, zig-zag lines etc.

☺   Pavement chalking provides lots of opportunities for practising early literacy skills – see Chapter 14 ('Books and Reading') for more ideas.

☺   Chalk different shapes onto the ground and encourage your child to jump onto the requested shape after saying 'ready…steady…go'. Start with only one shape, then add new ones, one at a time. Vary this with activities such as requesting your child to 'put the bean bag on the square/circle' etc. To add further receptive language skills, move on to presenting a choice, for example, bean bag, teddy, brick and chalk further shapes in different sizes and colours. You might then ask your child to 'Put teddy on the small circle' or 'Put bean bag on the yellow triangle'. Continue to use 'ready…steady…go' and rewards where necessary (verbal or otherwise). Remember some children with autism really don't like over enthusiastic shrill voices. Be aware if this is the case (he may actually see this as a reason *not* to co-operate). Try using bubbles, tickles, treats instead – see Chapters 2 and 3 for more ideas on positive reinforcement.

☺   As well as chalk, you can also draw on the ground with sand in a plastic bottle with a hole in, or with water in a squirty plastic bottle (those with a sports sipper cap are ideal).

Throwing balls at targets

☺   Fill a large plastic bowl/bucket or storage box with water (add coloured food dye for variety) and take turns throwing a ball into it. Try the following rhyme:

> Can Sally see the water in the box over there?
> Where is the water, Sally? Sally point where.

> Sally hold the ball and Sally throw now
> Splish splash splosh – look, Sally. Wow!

For your turn just change the words in the third line to, 'Mummy hold the ball and Mummy throw now.' For more rhymes see Chapter 8 ('Physical Activities').

☺ As well as throwing the ball into water try throwing it at a bell or wind chimes, or throwing it through a basketball net. (Fix this where it is achievable for your child.)

Sand play

If your garden is too small for a sand pit, or a pit is simply too overwhelming for your child, try filling a plastic storage crate with sand. (Remember to always use play sand in sand pits/boxes rather than ordinary builders' sand.) Wet sand might feel too uncomfortable so try dry sand at first and have a towel ready for him to wipe his hands on. Provide him with one or two containers, a small spade and a funnel. He might like to watch the sand flow from the funnel into an empty plastic drinks bottle, or try a sand toy, whereby the sand drives a wheel round. Only put enough articles for one activity at a time in with him. Your child might get a little *lost* in himself watching the sand run through his fingers. Allow him some time to do this then gently refocus him back to *joint* play.

☺ Build a series of sand castles. Then, after a count of three, let him jump on them one at a time.

☺ Provide a length of broom handle (with the end sanded smooth) for your child to draw shapes in the sand. You could create a greater surface area for this by putting a small amount of sand onto a large piece of wood or a stone slab. Try a talking commentary about what he is doing, for example, (Alex draws a random shape which looks like a letter), 'What will Alex draw? C, C, C, C. Alex draws a letter C – C for car and cat, Alex draws a letter C.' Try to make your child aware that what he is doing has an effect on what you say. Keep the commentary simple, not too loud and at first only comment on your child's spontaneous actions without directing them.

☺   If your child likes looking at road works, cranes, diggers etc., the sand pit/box is a great way to play realistically with them. Alternatively, for even more realism you could fill a box with clean dry potting compost which might have a more appealing texture than hard gritty sand.

Messy art

Outdoors is a particularly good place to work on a large scale – children with fine motor skill delays get less frustrated making big shapes than they do trying for example, to manipulate a paint brush on a small-scale drawing. Outside is also a great place to experiment with colour and texture without worrying about mess. All children can be particularly good at making a mess so take the paints outside and really enjoy it!

Check out Chapter 12 ('Being Creative') for art activities that can be done outside. In addition, try the following:

☺   Tape a large piece of lining paper (or wallpaper, reverse side up) to the side of a wall/shed/garage. With a decorator's paint brush let your child paint big shapes/long wavy lines or random marks. You might try drawing a simple shape like a cross at the opposite end of the paper to see if he will copy you.

☺   You could also allow him to dip a toy car into paint (water-based poster paint for easy clean ups!) and run it along the paper. Try doing this at your end of the paper (with a second car). Alternate making the car go fast and slow, straight and wavy (make appropriate noises to indicate what you are doing). See if your child will imitate what you are doing with *his* car.

☺   A decorator's small roller brush can also be a highly satisfying way of putting paint onto paper for a child who is having difficulty co-ordinating a brush or applying enough pressure.

☺   Experiment with different ways of getting the paint on the paper – dipping sponges in a tray of paint; flicking paint with fingers or brushes; hand, foot, even nose and tummy prints! Have a bowl of water, a wash cloth and a towel handy! On a very hot day have a painting session first, followed by a play in the paddling pool to make cleaning up less of a chore.

☺   When you have a day at the beach, don't forget to collect pebbles and shells to use in art activities and try the following. Roll out a thick layer of air-drying clay onto a piece of board or a plastic tray (smear a thin layer of petroleum jelly onto it first to help it release when it is dried). On a separate tray have your collection of beach treasure, perhaps with some additional pieces in it, such as glass nuggets, bits of twig, string etc. Take turns at pushing the objects into the clay and then leave the clay in the sun to dry. (Taking turns can be problematic for children with autism but is a vital skill to pursue, check Chapter 7 for ways to tackle turn-taking.) When the plaque is dry, if any items feel loose, take them out and glue them back into the impression they have made, with a dab of PVA or other suitable adhesive. Display the plaque where your child can see it, perhaps alongside his beach photos. Talking about past experiences using physical items such as shells, photos etc. helps your child to recall specific experiences and interpret their meaning (rather than just recalling a collection of sensory experiences and negative emotions). It also helps him understand a collection of words appropriate to a day at the seaside. This activity can also be used after a day walking in the woods (collect leaves, pebbles, twigs, seed heads, conkers, acorns etc.).

☺   Run a length of lining paper along the ground, weighted down each side with a large stone. Drop a medium-size rubber ball into a bowl of poster paint and take turns (see Chapter 7) rolling it to each other along the paper to make a coloured line. If your child is enjoying the activity but doesn't like the sensation of touching a ball covered in paint, let him wear mittens or plastic gloves (rolling a ball whilst wearing gloves is a good sensory exercise in itself).

Pet shops are good sources of rubber balls for this activity; many sell a variety with different textured surfaces. Even those with a bell inside help to capture attention.

Try the following rhyme:

> Ball in the paint, ball on the paper, roll roll roll to you
> Stop stop the rolling red ball, can you do it too?
> Ball in the paint, ball on the paper, roll roll roll to me
> What have we made ?…a wiggly red line
> Look, Tom – can you see?

☺   Try attaching a number of lengths of string (about 20) to a short section of broom handle with a piece of tape (like a small mop). Dip the ends into watered down poster paint and let your child mop the colour onto the pavement. Alternatively, use a less watery mix and let him drag the colour up and down a length of paper.

Balance and co-ordination games
Stepping stones

☺   Stepping stones can be anything from house bricks, carpet tiles, to pieces of wood, or circles chalked on the patio.

Judge how far apart and how high they should be according to your child's ability. To make it easier to differentiate the stepping stones from the ground, paint or chalk a bright colour onto them. As always, clear away any distractions so that all your child has to focus on are the stepping stones themselves.

☺   To add extra interest and learning potential, stick a picture onto each stone and ask your child to step on the picture of the...house, flower, cat. You might add to the game's potential by saying, 'Step on something that we live in' etc. Also try, number, letter and word stepping-stone games.

☺   Try covering half a dozen cork tiles with various textures – fur, silver foil, sandpaper, soft fabric, corrugated card, etc. Start by labelling them as your child steps onto them (with bare feet) – furry, smooth, rough, soft, bumpy etc. Keep the same label consistent. You might then play a 'ready...steady...go' game.

☺   Using the above set of tiles, make an identical set and play a matching game, for example, your child stands on the soft square and you say, 'Jump on something that feels the same' or 'Jump on something that feels different'. Tailor your language to your child's language level, i.e. you might just say 'same' or 'different'.

Balance beams

☺   A balance beam doesn't necessarily have to be off the ground – to start with, try joining two stepping stones with a length of ribbon, fabric, washing line – anything that creates a line he can follow between two points. You can then move on to balancing a piece of wood over two bricks and walking *along* it, stepping *over* it, crawling *under* it. Try the following rhyme:

> Follow me, follow me, where will Mummy go?
> Over here, over there, stepping to and fro
> Wibble wobble, wibble wobble, do you think I'll fall?
> Wibble wobble, wibble wobble...no not at all!

Don't forget to pretend to wobble! When it's your child's turn, just replace 'Mummy' with his name.

Outdoor adult role-play

Once they learn to imitate action, children with autism can often mimic adult actions in great detail. Copying actual everyday activities is something that has real meaning, is not ambiguous, does not require imaginative leaps and can be a fun and rewarding thing to do in its own right. With my own son, much of his spontaneous play involves toy versions of adult equipment – lawnmowers, cameras, mops/buckets etc. Needing props is part and parcel of this play and he struggles to improvise with imaginary props. Even now, if he pours pretend tea his teapot *must* contain real water. To *pretend* that he is pouring is simply not enjoyable enough to do. Playing outdoors offers lots of scope to do *real* activities, for example:

☺ Filling plant pots with soil and planting bulbs.

☺ Watering plants.

☺ Washing tables/chairs.

☺ Washing the car/bicycles.

☺ Washing the windows.

☺ Sweeping.

☺ Provide equipment for your child to use and be aware that he might want his own version of *everything* you use. So if you put detergent in your water, provide him with his own bottle (for economy, use a nearly empty bottle filled up with water). Don't forget to keep up a simple commentary about what you are doing whilst you do it. You might try a singing commentary as detailed in Chapter 6 ('Music').

Picnics

☺ Eating outdoors is a fun and exciting activity for all children. Children with autism, however, require some extra preparation to enjoy a picnic outside. Before embarking on a full-scale picnic, try to label the activity of eating outside a 'picnic' even if it is only eating a biscuit, sitting on a cushion in the garden. Non-autistic children have usually worked out the meaning of 'picnic' before they actually have one themselves, but again children with autism usually need to *experience* an event before they can understand its meaning. As well as giving it a verbal label, also use a picture card to represent 'picnic'. You might want to make two – one for teddies'/dollies' picnic and one for Tom's picnic (use your child's name).

☺ Start by introducing a pretend picnic game in the garden (communicating first that you are going to play 'teddy bears' picnic'). Gather together a few simple elements: a small blanket, two bears, plates, cups, round cardboard circles for cakes and a teapot. Even though I often emphasise the importance of realism, try to resist the temptation to use real food at first, as this can be too distracting and makes the significance of the other elements much less meaningful. Your child might be very likely to collect his cake, walk away and leave you to play picnics on your own! Only attempt five minutes concentration at first, during which you encourage him to imitate feeding the bears, making appropriate sounds etc. Use a simple script that can be repeated each time you play, for example:

'Today Fluffy and Blackie bear are having a picnic. Fluffy wants a biscuit. Can Joshua give him one? Now Blackie wants a cup of tea? What a lovely picnic – was that good bears?'

Once your child is engaging in the play you might want to introduce a plate and biscuit for him and you, but make sure the bears are fed their pretend food too!

☺   From this you could try moving onto a real picnic. (If sensory overload outside is too much, try a picnic in the living room first.) You might feel a 'picnic' is simply another name for eating a meal. However, the novelty of occasionally eating in this way helps your child:

- discover an activity that is enjoyable that eventually might include being away from the house and being with others

- experience an activity that he can relate to in stories and later on in discussions at school

- experience pretend play with toys that has an attractive and motivating element (food)

- take part in a situation where the potential for interaction is enhanced by engaging in a novel and pleasant experience

- enjoy an activity that siblings can get involved with.

Once again be aware of your own child's individual needs. Don't spring a collection of new foods on him hoping that the novelty of the situation means he'll eat differently – he probably won't and will get distressed. Don't overload him with language; keep sentences short and don't ask too many questions that you'll end up answering yourself. Say a sentence, for example, 'This is a big red tomato' and a little later repeat it. If your child is verbal you might want to test whether he has understood by asking, 'Is this a big blue tomato?'

Remember, if you try a picnic away from home, you might come against problems if you go along a familiar walk. On a regular route – perhaps where you feed ducks or go on the swings – your child may find it difficult to deviate from his usual activity. For this situation, find a novel location that he can come to associate with having a picnic, and then work on building in flexibility.

Big outdoor play equipment

It's common sense to visit parks at quiet times, to avoid as many stresses as possible. On a busy day you might conclude that your child dislikes this type of activity when all he really dislikes is the bombardment of noise and activity from other children. Take plenty of photos to use as picture prompts and to talk about later; also take something to wipe down slides and swings in case they are wet. (It's impossible to explain to a child with autism that he can't go on the swing because it's wet!) If your child is prone to knocks and bumps, pack some plasters or a bandage and keep his arms and legs covered.

Swings

Be aware of where your child is in terms of balance and co-ordination; just because his younger brother can use a plain swing doesn't mean your older child with autism no longer needs the bucket style. Like trampolining, swinging can provide a motion that is highly pleasant and can be used as a way to increase interaction. Likewise, to some children this type of motion can be distressing and uncomfortable – take your child's lead.

☺   If your child appears to enjoy the swing, you have a great tool to help you engage his attention. First, if you stand in front of him, he will find it hard to avoid eye contact and the swinging provides natural rhythm for you to use as part of your interaction. This is a good activity to use rhyme (but for this rhyme only if your child is in a bucket swing and has a hand free!).

> Swinging, swinging, Jacob in the sky
> Swinging, swinging, Jacob flying high
> Touch Mummy's hands with your flying knees
> Touch Mummy's hands with your flying toes
> Clap Mummy's hands with your flying hands
> Pat your head and touch your nose.

or

(To the tune of 'London Bridge is falling down')

> Katy Smith is swinging high, swinging high, swinging high
> Katy Smith is swinging high, swinging on a swing
> Katy's going to touch the sky, touch the sky, touch the sky
> Katy's going to touch the sky, swinging on a swing.

If you have a swing at home and your child has outgrown the bucket seat but is too unsteady for a regular seat, first shop around – bucket style seats vary in size. If all else fails, ask a local joiner to put one together for you – a simple square shape made from slats. Always make sure that your existing rope is strong enough to take your child's weight.

Slides

Slides can be easy for children with autism to co-ordinate (they may need extra supervision on the steps) and can provide a pleasant sensation.

☺ 'Ready, steady...go' games are natural to use on slides. Also try to encourage your child to repeat 'up' and 'down' as appropriate.

☺ For more able children, you can try some real challenges. Take some picture cards along with you and while your child is at the top of the slide ask him to tell you what the picture is before sliding down again. My own son finds this game very enjoyable – the tension of having to wait and the pleasure of getting something right are heightened in this situation.

☺ During all these activities, encourage your child to ask for 'more' or 'again' rather than just taking your hand back to the activity. Ask, 'More?' Give your child plenty of time to respond and accept any effort your child makes with praise and reward – 'Yes, Jack said more. OK then'. For a nonverbal child, create an opportunity for a communicative exchange by creating a long pause for him to respond with an intentional sound or gesture to indicate he wants another go.

Trikes, bikes and 'sit-ons'

Often young children with autism are drawn to these types of toys but simply haven't got the balance or co-ordination to control them. Rather than riding the tide of tantrums, simply remove them out of sight and re-try at six-monthly intervals. If your child has outgrown the toddler versions by the time his balance is developed enough to manage them try a specialist large tricycle (see the back of the book for details) or an ordinary bicycle with substantial stabilizers.

Trampolines

For older children who really enjoy trampolining there are outdoor trampolines available that can be permanently left in the garden (if the garden is large enough). Smaller children will enjoy the portable trampolines (with a handle bar), which are widely available for children up to six years. Remember to secure the base of these outside as they can be unstable. For a very safe option try sinking a small exercise trampoline into the ground. Dig a hole big enough for the trampoline to sit in flush with the ground. You might want to fix boards around the inside of the hole to secure the sides. This is ideal for children who are likely to fall or for older children. Don't forget to check out schools, play schemes and sports halls for trampoline sessions which allocate time for special needs' children.

To engage your child in interaction with you, try doing the following as they bounce:

☺   Clap or count in time to the bounces.

☺   Play 'stop and go' games. Announce; 'Ready, steady…bounce' and encourage your child to wait for the word 'bounce', after a few bounces, announce 'Ready, steady…stop' and physically encourage him to stop. You might also try using a gestural or visual signal to indicate stop and go, for example a 'clap' or lifting both arms up for 'go' and down for 'stop'. Try jumping on the floor next to your child and stopping and starting with him – make him aware that you are playing too!

☺   Play his favorite music on a tape player outdoors for him to bounce to. Try stopping and starting it so he has to listen and stop bouncing when the music stops.

☺   Try the following rhyme, recite it slowly in time with his bouncing:

> Charlie's bouncing on the trampoline
> How many bounces have there been?
> Stop now, Charlie count again
> One, two, three, four, five, six, seven, eight, nine, ten!

Or hold your child's hands as he jumps and recite the following – make him jump high and low as you tell/sing the rhyme.

> Once day in the sunshine Susan bounced high
> Jumped one two three and f...l...e...w...in the sky.
> Landed back down, bounced low low low
> But the bounces started to grow grow grow
> Bigger and higher they grew and grew
> Till she jumped in the sky and away she...flew!

Tunnels, play tents and cubes

This type of play equipment can be very versatile for indoor and outdoor play. The physical, 'no rules' nature of this type of play means children on the autism spectrum have less difficulty understanding what to do. Try the following:

Tunnels

☺ As your child crawls through the tunnel, pat the surface on the outside. See if he will pat the inside against your hand.

☺ The rigid rings that hold play tunnels together can be hard on the knees, especially to a child sensitive to physical sensations. Try cushioning the floor of the tunnel with a blanket if he is reluctant to crawl through. Also try different textures to crawl over, such as bubble wrap or fur fabric.

☺ See if your child will pat a balloon or roll a ball through the length of the tunnel.

☺   Let him take a torch into the tunnel or try shining one in from the outside. See if he will touch where the light lands.

☺   Play tunnels are perfect for 'peek-a-boo' games. Sit at the side of the entrance rather than at the front so that your child has to come right out and look for you.

☺   Play tunnels are also great for involving siblings in this style of play. Let the sibling stand upright inside the tunnel and pull it down with a 'boo!'.

☺   Some tunnels have clear panels which opens up even more possibilities. If putting your face against the panel makes your child pull away, try using a teddy or soft toy initially. Remember to create an opportunity for your child to indicate that he wants the game to continue by creating a 'long pause' and waiting for his response.

Play tents

Play tents (the pop-up variety) don't have to take up much room when stored and can be used for lots of uses. Try the following:

☺   Practice ringing a doorbell or knocking on the door for your child to open the entrance to the tent and say, 'Hello'. See if he will copy a short dialogue such as; 'Hello, would you like a cup of tea?' Use a real bell or a piece of wood for an authentic sound.

☺   Once again, play tents have a great potential for 'peek-a-boo'-style playing.

☺   For a child capable of some imaginative play, try 'play houses'. Provide a pillow and blanket for 'the bedroom' and play kitchen equipment.

☺   A child that isn't responsive to reading or playing a particular game may do so in the novel confines of the play tent. Experiment with a variety of activities. It may be that the tent cuts out external distractions and allows him to concentrate. It will be hard on your knees but worth a try!

Play cubes

☺   Pop up play cubes again have good 'peek-a-boo' potential – your child (or yourself!) can sit in the bottom and pop up through the hole with arms outstretched, on the count of three.

☺   Your child might simply love being picked up and put into the cube – encourage an interaction with a rhyme:

> What does Gemma want – up up up?
> Where do you want Mum to put put put?
> Up in the air…ready…wheeeeee!!
> Down in the cube with a 1, 2,…3!

Encourage your child to finish each sentence with you and pause for him to indicate if he wants more.

☺   Pop up cubes can be used as easy targets for throwing balls and bean bags – see Chapter 8 ('Physical Games and Activities') for lots of throwing ideas.

Outdoor play in winter weather

Autumn and winter can be fun times of the year for children to be outdoors. Children with autism may indeed prefer it cool and children that tend to fall more often can be cushioned in lots of warm clothing.

Heaped up dry leaves can be great fun. Try the following:

☺   Listening to the crunching sound they make as you walk through them.

☺   Play 'ready…steady…go' games for jumping into and throwing dry leaves.

☺   Let your child drop a handful and watch them flutter to the ground.

☺   If you regularly go on the same walk, take lots of photos at different times of the year so that you can look at the pictures and talk about what happens to the leaves. Try taking a series of pictures of one tree in particular. Looking at a real tree that your child has seen himself will make understanding the seasons more meaningful than just looking at books. Make your own scrap book with the photos and stick actual leaves in it – don't forget to include a picture of your child next to the tree.

☺   Whenever you are outdoors give your child a verbal and/or picture label for the weather. Let him see, touch (and even taste) frost and snow. Give it a consistent label – if you use the word 'frost' don't then use the words 'ice' or 'cold' or even 'frosty' until you are sure he understands what it means. Likewise if you use the word 'wind' don't then say 'gales', or 'blustery'.

Leaving footprints in snow is a satisfying activity for all children:

☺   Play follow the leader. Enlist the help of another adult to hold your child's hand and follow you through the snow. Stand back and look at the footprints you have made; try to retrace them.

☺   Squirt water and food colouring or watery poster paint from a detergent bottle into the snow and draw big shapes.

☺   Water the snow with a watering can and watch it melt.

☺   Once again take photos or even camcorder footage of the snow so that you can look at and talk about it at any time of the year – revisiting experiences using pictures like this is much easier for your child to understand than just using language. By talking about and looking at events after they have happened you can increase his understanding and steer his memories into positive ones rather than something that might have actually been anxiety-inducing for him at the time.

Other useful outdoor equipment includes windmills, wind chimes, streamers and ribbons. Be aware that for some children, items like these can help motivate them to interact with you and for others they may be so visually or aurally satisfying that they pull your child away from interaction. Observe and react accordingly.

Chapter 10

Water Play

Autism and water

Like music, water can often have a powerful effect on children with autism. They may be strongly drawn to the sight and sound of running taps, be mesmerized by light rippling on the surface of puddles, ponds and lakes, or become hysterically distressed by the sound of flushing toilets, the rush of the sea or the feel of even the slightest droplet of water on their skin. As with music, the goal is to harness the positive attractive qualities of water to use as a tool in interactive play whilst helping desensitize your child to those aspects of water that are stressful and unpleasant for him.

Problems and solutions

Sensitivity to the feel of water on the skin

Some children cannot bear the feel of water on their skin, which has obvious practical problems as well as hindering the possibilities of water play. I would suggest trying water play in a totally new context, away from bowls and bathrooms associated with washing.

Try putting a tray with a shallow lip on a table; protect surrounding areas or attempt this outdoors. Fill the tray with tepid water and a few marbles, and encourage your child to move the marbles around – he might only need to get the tips of his fingers wet at first. Alternatively, place a few edible treats that are OK to go in water, for example, currants, or give the water some taste with a little fruit juice added and let him dip his fingers in and lick them. Show him there is a towel nearby to dry his hands on.

Don't force his hands into the water and in the meantime keep essential washing as stress-free as possible by using flannels/wet wipes.

Note that many children with autism hate the sound of hot air dryers in public lavatories – they may scream at having their hands washed not because they hate the water but because they are afraid of the dryer!

Water obsessions

Alternatively, other children are driven to jump and sit in all available puddles, head to the bathroom wherever they may be, to play with taps and water, and will run the tap at home continually. If this is the case, at least there are no sensitivity issues to deal with! You will, however, have to be vigilantly structured in your water play otherwise the sensations your child is receiving from solitary water play may be so pleasurable to him that they help him pull back into his autistic aloneness, which is the polar opposite of what you are trying to achieve.

Limit the amount of time he plays with taps by use of a timer. If the sound of a bell timer is unpleasant for him try a *visual* clock timer (for details see references at the back of the book).

If activities like tap-running are highly pleasurable they may used as rewards/re-inforcers (as described in Chapter 4) after an amount of structured play. Communicate to your child (preferably by use of a picture card) that he can play with taps after a specific activity (again illustrated by a picture card).

Individual example: Katherine

Katherine adored all types of water play and although this meant her mum had an easy and available play activity to engage her in, it was often difficult to encourage her to interact or even make eye contact during these times. She resisted her mum 'interfering' or trying to direct her play. Her mum felt that letting her play with water was becoming an easy option to keep her quiet for a while but was not helping her in any other ways. Katherine's play with water had an obsessive and repetitive quality about it – she would repeatedly fill a plastic beaker with water at the sink then walk over to the bath and pour it in, time after time.

Katherine's mum decided that playing with water was so pleasurable to her that she would use the water play as a reward for another activity (still involving water) that had more learning potential. Katherine's mum put a small plastic table inside the bath and placed a shape sorter (an activity she knew Katherine could already do) on the table. She drew a picture of the shape sorter on one card and a picture of a beaker and a tap on another and held them up in front of Katherine saying 'shape first then water'. There was some objection at first but eventually she went over to the sorter and popped a shape in the correct aperture. Her mum immediately gave her the beaker saying; 'Yes, good work'. While Katherine filled and emptied the beaker, her mum took the opportunity to try to create a space for her to communicate – when the beaker was full, her mum put her hand over the top and said; 'Wait!…ready…steady…go!' She would leave a long pause before the word 'go' for Katherine to either attempt the word or make eye contact. After a while Katherine stopped objecting and appeared to enjoy the anticipation of her reward even more.

The following day her mum changed the activity slightly and just put the shapes on their own out on the table and asked Katherine to give her the 'square'. Katherine put the shape in the beaker and poured it into the bath – she had created her own new version of the game which her mum went along with. Each play session her mum produced different activities for her to do (being mindful that they were likely to get wet!). After each activity Katherine was always rewarded with her beaker and water play. The water play activity had now taken on a more interactive and learning quality and Katherine herself appeared to enjoy this more than simply repetitively pouring.

Enjoying water play indoors

Bath times can be a valuable opportunity to interact with your child. If he enjoys bathing, then you already have him in a relaxed accessible state of mind to try the play ideas below.

If bathing is a stressful and unpleasant experience, try the following:

- Check to see that it is not just the prospect of hair washing that is stressing your child. Many children with autism hate this necessity and bathing exposes them to the possibility. Try creating two picture cards of a shampoo bottle and draw a red cross over one of them. For those days where your child *will* be having his hair washed, show the picture of the shampoo bottle and then a picture of a treat that you know he will enjoy (favourite video, box of paper to rip, packet of crisps etc.). For bathing where there will be *no* hair washing show him the bottle with the cross through it and verbally reinforce by saying, 'No hair wash'. If it is simply hair washing that stops him enjoying his bath then once he understands this will not happen he can calm down and enjoy playing. Never spring hair washing on a child that hates it in the hope that it will all be over and done with quickly. You will only raise his anxiety levels about anything to do with washing and bathing as well as undermine his trust in you. If shampoo is the terror, try just using wet flannels, or even washing his hair out of the bath with wet flannels. For little girls who hate hair washing, a shorter style means less washing and brushing stress!

- If it is simply the *feel* of water that he hates try reintroducing bathing. Fill the bottom of the bath with just a few centimetres of water and let your child keep on his clothes, but remove his shoes and socks. Work at getting him to retrieve something out of the bath first with his hands and then see if he will step into it – don't worry if he gets the rest of his clothes wet; just take off more each time. Allow him to get used to the feel of bathing at his own pace. Gradually over the course of around a week he will, with any luck, be coaxed back into the bath. During this time you can keep your child clean with washcloths or wet wipes, but do this away from the bathing sessions. Children with autism can be sensitive to temperatures. Adults in particular usually enjoy a bath temperature hotter than most children find pleasant. If your child cannot communicate to you that the water is too hot this only fuels his distress.

Bath time play

☺   Your child can play with water in the bath *without* actually sitting in it! Try placing a large plastic box in the bath – if it is too low for your child to reach, place it on a small stool or onto another plastic crate. Fill it with warm water and experiment with temperatures, bubbles and food colour to see what particularly delights him. Remember that your child and all surrounding areas *will* get wet – an old shower curtain on the floor will save most puddles (cover it with towels to avoid slipping). Try dropping different objects into the water – marbles, stones, polystyrene chips, cotton reels, buttons, shells, coins. Offer your child a choice of three or four objects to drop in and take turns. Provide a simple commentary about what you are doing, for example:

> 'Sam's turn, a stone! Ready, steady, plop – look it's sunk!'

> 'Mum's turn, a ping pong ball! Ready, steady, splash – look it's floating!'

Try to use the activity for turn-taking and language (receptive and expressive) acquisition. Remember to always try to create a space, a long pause for your child to make a communicative gesture. He may want you to continue a particular activity or he may want to use something else – respond to anything that seems to be an intentional attempt to communicate.

☺   Practise pouring water from teapots into cups, from one beaker into the other and using funnels. Be aware of what might frustrate your child (i.e. if a container has a neck too small for him to manage).

When your child is *in* the bath try the following:

☺   Provide a wide wooden board to fit across the bath (a batten fixed to one edge will secure it). Your child can then comfortably pour water in and out of containers at eye level. Try to make his play meaningful – if he pours water into a cup, pretend to drink it! Don't provide too many containers/jugs/bottles at once, especially if these are likely to be lined up or stacked.

☺   Pour water from a jug held high up – hold it well away from him at the other end of the bath – and see how he responds. If he likes it, pause and encourage him to say, indicate, or make a gesture (a look or a noise) to indicate 'more' or 'go' after 'ready, steady…'.

☺　Try sending a wind-up bath toy to and fro. Choose a chunky design that he will be able to manage.

☺　Get in with your child for some good face-to-face fun. Let him pour water over your hair and exaggerate your responses to make him laugh, or have a squirty water session using animal squirters.

☺　Wash mits shaped like glove puppets have lots of possibilities for 'now you see me, now you don't' type games.

☺　Bath crayons and coloured soap that are specially designed for children to paint in the bath also have good imitation possibilities. Try sticking a safety mirror to the side of the bath and put a coloured dot on your child's face. Let her look in the mirror and say, for example, 'Fiona's blue cheek/nose/ear…point to Fiona's blue cheek' etc. See if your child can put a mark on your face where you request. This is a good play activity to encourage a sense of identity. Children with autism often have problems with attaching a sense of belonging to their own physical bodies, as well as problems with sense of self and identity. All play activities that encourage your child to acknowledge physical aspects of himself as well as his own emotional responses and behaviour help him build a sense of who he is.

Table-top water play

☺　Drop ice cubes one by one, taking turns, into a shallow transparent dish and see what happens. Try pressing them down into the water and watching them bob up again. For extra interest, freeze pieces of fruit into the cubes or freeze blocks of juice so your child can try holding and licking them. Again, the extreme temperature may be uncomfortable for him to touch; if this is the case, use a spoon but tempt him to touch the blocks when you can. Try the following rhyme to engage his attention:

> Cold, cold ice in the water…splash
> Watch it crack and pop and crash
> Here comes another…count with me
> Ready to splash, one, two,…three! (encourage your child to say 'three')

☺   Try freezing a small plastic toy into an ice cube, then place it on a plate in a warm room and watch it melt. Keep going back to the plate, saying, 'Look, melting'. You can try bringing a snowball in in winter and doing the same thing.

☺   Using an old washing-up bowl, try adding either oil-based paints or cooking oil and swirling it over the surface of the water to make patterns. You can also try blowing over the water with a straw to make it move. If you use paints, take a sheet of paper and rest it on the surface of the water – lift it off for a marbled paint effect.

☺   Place a mirror in the bottom of a bowl of water and encourage your child to look into it. Play at rippling the water to change the reflection.

A splashy sorting game

☺   Place two different coloured plastic storage containers in front of your child and pour a little water into the bottom of one of them (enough water to make a decent splash when an object is thrown in!). Place in front of your child a plastic duck, dolphin, pig, horse, sheep (be inventive with the plastic toys you have at home). Sort the objects into those that live in water and those that live on land by doing the following:

Holding up the duck, say, 'Benjamin – does this live in water?'. Give your child time to answer but then prompt the answer yourself after a while by saying, 'Yes...a duck lives in water! Ready, steady...go' and throw the duck into the water box. The reward of throwing the object is motivating for your child and should capture his attention. You may have to provide the answers for him for the first few sessions; after that you might want to add some new objects or try a different category of water/land objects, for example, transport.

☺ Even though it can be messy, after a meal allow your child to help you wash the pots or provide a bowl and soapy water for him to wash some plastic dishes – he might prefer to wash real plastic dishes/jugs etc. than toy ones. A two-step ladder to reach the sink is useful for lots of activities.

Outdoor water play

Like the bath, the paddling pool can be a useful means of encouraging interaction. Try the following:

☺ Provide your child with a fishing net and see if he can scoop up a ball out of the water – provide a big enough ball so that the activity is not too difficult. This is a good activity to develop hand–eye co-ordination skills. Try having a net each and a race to see who can catch the ball first. To increase his motivation for this activity use a favourite toy/object (if it's waterproof) or reward him with a treat or reinforcer each time he catches something in the net.

☺ Alternatively, make fish from ping pong balls with eyes/mouths drawn on in waterproof marker pen and see how many you can scoop into your nets.

☺   If you have a number of ball pit balls, fill the paddling pool with these and see if your child can retrieve an object from underneath them.

☺   Some children adore the sensation of splashing in puddles. If the weather isn't hot enough for paddling pools, try splashing (wearing Wellington boots) in plastic trays/boxes. If this is highly enjoyable, use it as a reward for another activity (see Chapter 9 for outdoor play ideas).

☺   There are many attachments in the shape of different characters that can be attached to a hose pipe, which is then secured to the ground. When switched on, the hose pipe will randomly sprinkle whatever gets in its path! In very hot weather this can be a pleasantly cooling and fun activity. Siblings in particular will enjoy joining in with this one. Do be wary if your child's sensitivities mean he finds the water unpleasant. Try the following:

See if your child will run to you through the water, playing 'ready, steady, go…'; he may be willing to hold a sibling or another adult's hand.

Run together to retrieve something – give your child a choice of three objects and request he collects, for example, 'the spade'.

Swimming

Many children with autism learn to enjoy the swimming pool and it can be a valuable activity in which they can participate at the same level as their peers. As with all children, it is best to introduce your child to the swimming pool at as early an age as possible; however, for children with autism this also needs to be done gradually and gently. You may already have given up on swimming if your child seems to get distressed, has tantrums and generally makes the whole experience unpleasant for all concerned. This may not be because he doesn't like the water! Swimming pools are a cacophony of strange smells, a general noise level that doesn't go away, showers, shrieking, dressing, undressing and being dried – all of which can be distressing to child with sensory processing problems. This doesn't mean that it isn't worth persevering – if he can start to enjoy the activity, it opens the way for further interaction opportunities, is a means to expend excess energy and a valuable skill for a child whose sense of danger may not be as finely tuned as that of his non-autistic peers.

Check beforehand when is the quietist time for you to visit and start with small ten minute visits, – stand in the foyer, sit in the cafe, look at the spectators. Let your child get used to the sounds and smells and follow the trip with something pleasant that he enjoys doing. At home, look at books about swimming and practice wearing armbands. When you feel you are ready to go properly, have your own costume on under your clothes so that your child doesn't have to wait too long for you to be ready. Stay in the water for only ten minutes for the first few sessions – don't wait until your child starts to get agitated before you get out. Make sure you leave on a happy note (warning him first that you will be going soon). In the water, hold onto your child and don't push him to let go until he feels safe.

Gradually introduce the following activities:

☺   Holding his hands, get your child to jump whilst you walk backwards slowly. Make this a fun activity rather than an enforced exercise in learning to swim. Try the following rhyme:

> Bouncing in the water
> Jumping in the sea
> Ready for a big splash
> One, two…(long pause for a communicative gesture)
>   …three!

☺   If there are steps (as opposed to a ladder) into the pool, try jumping off the bottom step and gradually moving higher up until your child is ready to jump in off the side.

☺   Take along a child's watering can and play at pouring water onto each other's shoulders, or take a small ball and try to hold it under the water. Play a 'ready, steady, go' game – make your child wait for you to let the ball bob back up to the surface and encourage him to say 'go'.

☺   Don't forget to check with your pool or local support group to see if there are any special needs' sessions. These are often staffed by people experienced in working with children (and adults) with a variety of learning disabilities. Air beds, dinghies and inflatables may be provided or you may be allowed to bring your own. Try taking a small inflatable boat or air bed and pushing your child between yourself and another adult. Encourage your child to request 'fast' or 'slow', 'more', 'go' and 'stop'.

After the swim, don't pursue the shower unless your child enjoys it. A toweling robe with a hood may help him block out some of the noise and make him feel more secure. The promise of a treat/snack at the end may help him focus on getting dressed and reinforce his interpretation of the event as being enjoyable.

Chapter 11

Television Potential

Television - why?

It may seem inappropriate to include a piece about television in a book on play and interaction. However, TV *can* be an exceedingly useful tool:

- Television can be an excellent non-intrusive teaching medium. It can show images and concepts that are very difficult to explain to a language-impaired child and it doesn't demand the level of interaction that learning one-to-one does. Obviously TV is just a supplement to daily learning.

- Children with autism are usually 'visual thinkers', taking in, processing and learning lots of information from their 'visual channel'. Television is obviously a highly visual medium. For more information about visual thinking and autism, try reading *Thinking in Pictures* by Temple Grandin (see references at the back of the book)

- Television is 'controllable' – volume can be adjusted and images can be shown in short bursts at your child's control. Camcorder footage of 'real' events enables your child to re-play experiences where he can adjust the sensory input and can stop and start at will.

- Enabling your child to watch TV allows you to have a rest, knowing that your child isn't just absorbed in self-stimulatory behaviour, or worse still destructive/harmful behaviour.

- The repetitive possibilities of videos are appealing – your child may want to watch the same video many times. If the subject matter is chosen carefully so that it includes a learning element, then an obsessive and 'autistic' behaviour can introduce learning whilst being soothing and enjoyable.

- TV gives you breaks to set up new activities, make important phone calls etc.

- It gives your child a physical break and helps him to sit still for a period. Something he finds particularly engaging can help his concentration skills and be used as a starting point for supplementary learning.

- If your child is ill, it can take his mind off how he feels and keep him occupied.

Common problems and possible solutions

Watching the same video/episode over and over again and being highly resistant to new ones

Try the following:

☺   Make an *audio* tape of a new video and play it quietly in the background while your child is absorbed in something he enjoys or while you are out and about in the car. Try playing the sound track to something like a musical-based Disney video. Once he's used to how it sounds, introduce the video indirectly, in the following way:

This is best done with two people for maximum distraction! Occupy your child in a game of rough and tumble (if that's what he enjoys), dancing, hide and seek, or any other highly engaging game. Whilst one of you is doing this, the other puts on the new video without the child seeing and with the sound on low. Gradually increase the sound with one of you blocking the view to the television (not in a way that draws attention to it!). Follow your child's lead – if he recognizes the sound he may slow down the game and try to watch, or he may work out what's happening and begin to protest. If this happens, increase the physical play to distract him – he will probably continue to be aware of what's going on with the TV. If your child continues to object, only play the video for a few minutes at a time. Once the video no longer feels completely new he may start to accept it being on in the background, maybe with the sound off. Use lots of rewards/encouragement but be warned – choose the video carefully. He may well only watch this one for the next few weeks until you go through the same procedure all over again with the next new video!

☺ Choose a video that is slow paced, has minimum language or is still easy to understand without the sound on. Fast-paced action cartoons and films will require too much 'decoding' for your child to benefit. A familiar character from a book may be a good place to start. If you've never seen the video before, watch it with your child and have the remote control ready; some seemingly gentle videos might have something that your child finds highly disturbing. You might like to try something very repetitive with learning potential, such as an alphabet or counting video. Some children may be resistant to a video at home but watch it in a different setting, such as at Grandma's or a friend's. Arrange for a particular video to be playing before you arrive. My own little boy absolutely refused to watch a new video he had had in the collection for over a year. However, when he saw it playing at a friend's house he later dragged it out at home and demanded to watch it and it became a firm favourite!

Insisting on watching videos on fast forward

☺   This is a tricky one but apparently quite a common visual 'stim' (self-stimulation behaviour). Luckily I haven't had this problem with my own son but I would be tempted to tackle it using a short-exposure method followed by a reward i.e. requiring your child to tolerate a burst of, for example, five seconds (played at normal speed) at a time, followed by a treat/tickles/favourite toy. You may feel that the activity of watching videos on fast forward is so pleasurable to your child that it can be used as a reward/re-inforcer in itself for tackling a more demanding activity, or for even watching five minutes of normal-speed playing. Try creating a picture prompt for TV played at normal speed and one for fast speed as follows:

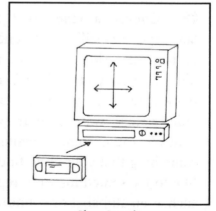

Fast Speed   Slow Speed

Limit the amount of time the video is played on fast forward by using a timer with a bell or a visual timer (see the back of the book for details).

Alternatively, you may feel this is an inappropriate activity altogether and prefer to concentrate on very small bursts of normal speed playing.

☺   If you don't object to the activity but want to work at 'normal speed' TV-watching, try keeping just one video that he is allowed to watch on fast forward. Your child might tolerate a new regime with a different video rather than his favourite one.

☺   Try to explore whether visual or auditory sensitivities might be causing the behaviour. Experiment with the sound/light levels in the room – observe whether he wants to do this if he's tired, stressed or bored.

Insisting on the TV being on constantly but not paying any real attention to it

Many parents in my survey reported that their children just liked a continuous background noise and often had the television on all day – without actually paying it much attention. My own son became like this with audio tapes and I could only conclude that the constant noise was a form of security (by repeating the same songs over again) and possibly helped to counteract his sound sensitivities.

He still wakes up in the night and if something is bothering him he asks for 'music on' (the same tape). During the day, however, I found that the more structured his time became, the more we could allocate specific times for listening to tapes. We even have a picture card for listening to music, which is a specific activity for him rather than simply an obsessive ritual. Working along these lines then it may be useful to try the following:

☺   Introduce a picture card with a TV drawn on it and when your child indicates that he wants it on, ask him to do one other thing first, for example, listen to a story, eat his breakfast, get dressed. Aim to put the TV on 15 minutes later each day. Keep adding more activities for him to do until you arrive at an acceptable time for it to go on (the last two hours before bed, for example). Try slow gradual change at your child's pace, and provide something to occupy him as an alternative. If the *sound* of the TV is the most important thing to him, try moving onto audio tapes or background radio noise first, or gradually lowering the volume until he adjusts to the quiet. Don't be overly rigid; if your child is tired, unwell or stressed and simply needs the comfort of either his favourite video, or just the knowledge that the TV is on, don't deny him it. Work on reducing TV time when he is feeling up to the challenge.

Many uses for the camcorder

The camcorder can be another useful piece of technology to help your child. If you own one don't just keep it for special occasions:

☺   Video footage of you interacting with your child can be a useful learning tool for yourself. If you are doing a daily structured learning session (detailed in Chapter 3), try taping one session a week or fortnight. Look at it with your speech and language therapist and see how your communication may be improved. Note which things worked and how you can build on them. Ask another adult to tape you in free play with your child or just set up the camcorder to capture your activities one afternoon/morning every couple of weeks. Watch it with a notepad and record what worked and what produced a negative response. Ask another adult to watch it with you – he or she may see something you missed!

☺   Video footage is an honest and objective record of your child's progress. It can help in the early days to get the right diagnosis and be used to demonstrate to professionals the problems that you might be encountering. Don't just tape your child playing on his own; include his interactions with you, other children and adults.

☺   If your child attends a playgroup/nursery and changes his behaviour if you stay with him (for example, clings to you, demands to go home), then, if someone in the group is prepared to film your child, you can have a fly-on-the-wall view of how he copes in your absence. Please note, the group may have to get the consent of all the other parents before they can film, as it is possible that their child will also be caught on the video.

☺   Often when children with autism are out and about on trips they are bombarded by an over-abundance of sensory stimulation, which inhibits their ability to take on, understand and learn from the experience. Recording highlights and playing them back helps your child to return to the experience again in the comfort and security of his home environment and offers many opportunities to learn about what he saw (for example, a trip to a zoo, a family outing) and to reinforce the idea that the experience was pleasant. If you talked about and explained what was happening to your child at the time the chances are he probably took in only a fraction of what you said. Video footage allows you to have a second chance at explaining events to your child in a context where he is more likely to be receptive and understand what you are saying. Revisiting real life experiences in this way also helps to give meaning to your child's participation by piecing together what may have seemed like a jumble of chaos at the time.

☺   If you are having difficulty explaining a particular behaviour to the professionals in charge of your child's care, film your child and explain as you are filming what circumstances led to the problem; it may be self-harming, extreme distress, or destructive behaviour. Try to film a few incidences of the same behaviour – this way you can be sure that the professionals know exactly what you mean. It's often difficult to explain the different 'quality' to an autistic child's behaviour, especially when well-meaning people say things like, 'All toddlers have tantrums' or 'He's just trying to manipulate you'. If your gut feeling is that this is not right and needs dealing with, let the professionals know exactly what you mean. It may be that you are reading this book even though your child doesn't have a diagnosis, you may be waiting for a referral or be at the start of the 'system' – a video diary of your child's behaviour at home playing, out and about with other children and the behaviours that are causing you concern will help decide if indeed he is on the autism spectrum and what steps to take next.

Video modelling

Video modelling means recording a demonstration of, for example, playing with a toy, so that your child can watch and imitate. Using the video to do this rather than doing it in front of him has many advantages:

- It removes the stress of you touching his toy in front of him.

- It can be played at a volume your child finds comfortable.

- It can be repeated many times and stopped and started under your child's control.

- It is less direct and obtrusive for your child.

- It allows you to really think about what language to use, what speed to talk at and what 'scripts' you feel would be useful for your child to learn.

Look at Chapter 13 ('Creating Imaginative Play Sequences') for ideas on how to set up a play sequence and work out a 'script'. There are lots of activities you can 'model':

☺ Play sequences with toys, for example, teddies' tea party, train sets, pretend cooking etc.

☺ Drawing or painting – for example, a simple picture that you know is not beyond your child's ability. Talk through choosing the right colour, how to wash your brush between colours (and dry off on a piece of sponge).

☺ Counting beads as you thread them onto laces.

☺ You could enlist the help of another child and tape the two of you talking. This might include entering the room and saying, 'Hello, my name is…', 'What's your name?', 'How old are you?' etc. Or tape yourself playing a 'turn-taking' game with your child's siblings (see Chapter 7, 'Turn-Taking in Play').

Setting up a video modelling session takes some time and needs at least two people. Have in mind what your 'script' will be – talk slowly and clearly but don't sound 'robotic'. Like all your play activities, keep the 'stage' clear of clutter and the camera firmly focused on the activity/people concerned. Introduce the video in the ways described earlier and have the toys being played with in the video available to your child as he watches it. He may need to watch it a few times before he attempts to copy; he may just like to watch the video as an activity in its own right, which is equally fine.

Finally, if you do own a camcorder or have access to one, don't forget to keep a record of your child's general and ongoing development. Tape his structured learning sessions, his free play, his interactions when guests visit, your trips out to the park, holidays etc. For any child these are precious memories; for a special child these memories help him to piece together who he is – his identity – and give him a sense of his history. For you they are times to look back on in the future and see how far you've all come since the dark early days of diagnosis.

Chapter 12

Being Creative – Art and Craft

Why art?

Imagine having no spoken language, living in a world that doesn't seem to make sense, with little predictability, where others make every decision for you from what you will eat to when you will go to the toilet. Now imagine the satisfaction that making a mark on paper may have, to make that same mark consistently if you use the same action, to decide where on the paper, how big, what colour – imagine how it would feel to have some *control?*

My experience as an art and craft facilitator for adults with learning disabilities has always supported my conviction that creativity is a valuable outlet for self-expression in people whose language and/or physical movements are impaired. I don't mean self-expression in an 'arty' kind of way, but in the sense that '*mark making*' is an important means of acting purposefully upon the world around us. To have control over a tool and leave an image for others to see is a primitive and fulfilling action. Putting marks on paper can have the same tension-releasing quality as running or even screaming. Try it yourself – next time you're really angry, take a pen and some paper and scribble as hard and fast as you can – sit back and observe how you feel! Now think of the extra reasons why your child has cause to be angry. Art is not just about nice pictures – it's about processes that have a positive effect on well-being, whether it be a deliberate act of control, a release of tension, a deeply relaxing meditative effect, or the communication of thoughts into pictures for the world to see.

The obstacles between art and your child

As usual, providing children with autism with materials and encouragement is often not enough. The materials themselves may be a major distraction – some children may be overwhelmed by the smell, feel and sight of lots of different colours. Others may have compulsions to eat the paint or rip the paper or flick paint around the room. Others may resist direction of any kind or have problems holding brushes that lead to frustration and tantrums – enough to make any parent wearily give up after a few attempts. However, if these problems can be worked around, painting provides a joint activity with rich potential, a time to share communicating and learning about colours and images and a great way to have fun!

Gaining attention by being indirect

Involving your child in any art activity requires a certain amount of prolonged direction which children with autism prefer to push away, (literally, quite often!). I found *initially* with my son that it was best to resist the urge to continually request and prompt (verbally), rather to approach painting in the least invasive way possible – no announcement. I simply quietly gathered together the materials (usually while my son was watching television and was distracted). Once his video had stopped I would then start working on my own – painting as if for my *own* pleasure. Gradually he would approach the table and make a few marks on the paper I'd left for him. After a few sessions conducted like this, he occasionally would initiate the activity himself by bringing me the paints or choosing the picture prompt if it was amongst those offered for him to choose. Sometimes, if the activity was scheduled as part of the day's picture diary, he would only be motivated by the prospect of a following reinforcer (a preferred activity or treat) – but the fact remained that he had become motivated! These sessions were *very* short indeed to begin with, but over time he will now tolerate more direction and remain focused for longer periods. This 'indirect' approach is a useful procedure to introduce any new activity for the first time without 'over loading' your child by invading his senses with new experiences.

If you haven't already read it, take a look at Chapter 2 ('Early Playing Skills: Gaining Attention and Sharing Space'). You know your own child best – he may already love paint and need no encouragement to start, but you might just need ideas for what to do to keep him on task, motivated and able to allow a level of direction. Alternatively, you may be having problems getting started because of sensory issues or problems with repetitive and rigid behaviour. Chapter 3 ('Structured Play') also looks a little deeper at the need for structure and the use of picture cards/prompts to communicate activities to your child. If your child is often quite 'accessible', you may want to begin with a picture prompt to get started, or you may choose an indirect non-invasive introduction – go with what you feel might work for your child and don't be afraid to abandon one approach in favour of another.

Getting started

- Prepare the room well so that your concentration is not on anything other than your child. Work in a room that can suffer a few spills, but protect the floor and furniture – in fact, covering all surfaces with dust sheets may help to minimize distractions by other things. Work away from the television and other toys that might compete for attention. Have a packet of wet wipes/flannels and a roll of kitchen towel at hand. If your child objects to an apron, don't force him; just don't put him in his best clothes that morning! You might like to add a few drops of washing-up liquid to paint before you use it, as this will help when it comes to washing it out of clothes and furnishings.

- If your child is unable to resist compulsively ripping the newspaper covering the table, cover the surfaces with old sheets instead. Better still, find a way to communicate to your child that after the session he can rip a whole paper into pieces (over the litter bin!). If he has difficulties understanding this, draw two simple pictures – a stick man painting on one piece of card and a stick man ripping paper on the other – and hold them up one after the other, saying, 'Paint first, then ripping'. Repeat this as often as it takes. The comforting and satisfying behaviour of paper ripping can be used as a reward or reinforcer and given an appropriate outlet. Tempting as it is to try to eradicate the behaviour altogether, the chances are your child will still indulge in this activity and satisfy his craving by ripping your important documents and papers instead!

- Look at the materials. What might your child find distracting? If repeatedly putting on and taking off pen tops and paint caps/lids is a problem, present him with pens without tops and paint in dishes.

- Start introducing one or two colours at a time – don't overwhelm him with choice.

- If licking the paint is a problem, make an edible paint with cornflower, water and food colouring. If you want to discourage licking so that you can move onto using real paint, try adding a little vinegar!

- Use big sheets of paper to work on – pieces of wallpaper lining are ideal. Only show your child one piece at a time so he doesn't get distracted by multiple sheets.

- If your child has an aversion to the feel of paint, provide a means whereby he can get it to the paper without touching, for example, using pieces of sponge that are chunky and easy to handle. Work on desensitizing him to such textures by providing bath paints that can be smeared onto the side of the bath or tiles (see the back of the book for where to find bath paints and crayons). A flat plank of wood resting over the bath is a great piece of equipment for all sorts of play. For extra security, screw battens underneath so it fits snugly without slipping (don't forget, the wood will need to be varnished).

- You can make edible (and pleasant-tasting) finger paints out of any food substance that will leave a mark – try blackcurrants (cooked, puréed and cooled) or chocolate cake frosting. Provide a tray and tools to draw patterns into the food and take prints of them by resting a piece of paper over the top. This is a good activity to help children tolerate paint-like substances on their hands.

- Provide yourself with a piece of paper at the same time and try drawing simple shapes, single lines or circles to see if you child will imitate you. Label your shapes as if labelling them to yourself – leave it for him to see and keep making the same mark over again. Resist the natural urge to provide a lot of verbal direction, unless he is comfortable for you to direct one task at a time for example, 'Paint on brush…a circle face…two eyes…a nose…a mouth…a face…good!'. If this level of direction is too much, try physical prompts and minimal speech, for example, point to your eyes and at the paper and just say 'eyes', 'nose' etc.

- Try copying your child's actions – make the same marks he does. If he uses the paint inappropriately (but not destructively), copy that too – put paint on *your* nose, dab the brush on your hand, shake out the paper. As well as attempting to pull him into the experience of your world occasionally slip into *his* too! Gain his trust by showing him that you are aware of his different experience and don't *always* want to stop or change it. After a while he may want to trust the idea of copying *your* actions anyway.

- Try singing a *commentary* about what you're doing, for example, 'Red paint on my brush goes round and round…' (sung to 'The wheels on the bus…'). Leave lots of pauses for your child to finish the song or indicate 'more'. Always be aware of creating opportunities for him to communicate.

- Keep initial sessions very short – one or two marks on paper followed by a rewarding activity or treat. It might seem an awful lot of preparation for 30 seconds of activity but once your child realizes that he's not in for a long slog he'll naturally lengthen the time he spends.

- Display the work in a prominent place for a few days and keep referring to it. Don't try to interpret a single stroke as 'A picture of Daddy'! – just keep repeating, for example; 'Joshua's painting! – I like that'.

- As your child becomes more familiar and relaxed with his painting sessions, add some variety so that he doesn't expect to just make the same blue line every day. Try the following:

    ○ Change the colours each session (don't just keep adding new ones – take some away too).

    ○ Rotate the materials – chunky crayons, felt tips, chalks, paint dabbers.

    ○ Vary the tools – stampers, brushes, sponges. Find out what your child seems most confident at handling. Try unconventional tools too, such as meat basters, decorators' brushes/paint pads and scrunched up fabric dipped in paint.

    ○ Try different combinations, for example, white paint/black paper, gold paint/red paper.

    ○ Experiment with the colour of the paper – stark white may be too reflective and disturb your child's vision. Be aware and responsive to any sensory difficulties he might have and work around them.

    ○ Start collecting together a box of everyday materials that you can recycle and use.

Art ideas

I would need a separate book to detail all the art activities you can try with your child, but this isn't what the chapter is about. It's about *finding a way* to motivate and enable a child with autism to join in the activity in the first place and using the experience to enhance communication and learning. Try the following art activities to get your imagination going and use them with the level of direction and/or motivation strategies that work best for *your* child:

☺   Simple stampers (decorators stamps are ideal) – if your child has trouble picking them up, stick an old cotton reel or empty camera film case to the back of the stamper as a handle, provide a tray to put the paint in and dip the stamp onto it. You may need to hold your hand over your child's or simply prompt him verbally or, better still, just touch his hand as a prompt. Stamping images can be used to help counting skills, hand/eye co-ordination and labelling. Try drawing empty squares onto the paper for your child to fit the stamp in. This challenges his ability to aim the stamp at the paper correctly and helps when it comes to counting the pictures. Also try good old potato prints, as well as mushrooms, broccoli and carrots.

☺   Use stamps to introduce sequences to your child. In a row from left to right, stamp a series of images, for example, elephant, car, elephant, car, elephant. Hold up the two stamps and ask your child to choose which one to use next.

☺   Colour some water with food colouring and encourage your child to blow through a straw into it. Demonstrate what happens when you blow, by having your own bowl and straw. Once you've whipped up lots of bubbles, rest a piece of paper over the top to create a print – very satisfying! You might prefer to use a transparent straw so that you can check he's blowing and not sucking!

☺   To encourage pre-writing skills, produce some cards with simple exercises on (for example, joining two dots with a straight line) and cover them with transparent book film. This can then be used as a dry-wipe board and is less flimsy and distracting than pieces of paper. Try making pairs of the same board so that you can demonstrate what to do on your own board. You might like to invest in an electric laminator if your child enjoys this kind of activity. You can also use it to laminate picture prompt cards and create schedules/star charts etc. Tailor the images to your own child's particular interests. For example, stick a photo of *your* car at one side of the card and draw a petrol pump at the other – encourage your child to join the two with a line. My own son has an 'electric-socket-and-plug interest' (carefully monitored for obvious reasons!). He was very eager to draw lines connecting the plug to the socket and this could then lead on to a simple discussion about safety and not touching sockets.

☺   Practise recognizing emotions by drawing various faces on paper plates. Stick a plastic spoon to the reverse side so that the plates can be held up in front of your (or teddy's!) face. Use them in your table-top learning sessions (see Chapter 3). Don't just label the pictures and leave it at that – try to give an example of what might make you happy/sad/cross. Use the faces when you are reading books. For example, when reading 'Goldilocks and the Three Bears' you could hold up the appropriate expressions, or use them when you're playing, for example, to reinforce the fact that teddy feels happy *when* he dances. Better still, throughout the day when your child expresses an emotion acknowledge it with a label, for example, 'OK, I know you're feeling angry' etc.

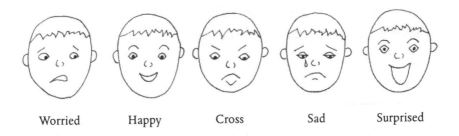

Worried   Happy   Cross   Sad   Surprised

☺   Because children with autism tend to have problems seeing images as a 'whole', help your child understand how a series of marks can represent an image by setting up the real object for him to see. For example, if you're drawing a teddy, set one up on the table and prompt him to choose colours. Show him (on your own paper) how the teddy's head, body and ears can be drawn as different size circles and his arms and legs can be single lines. If your child seems uninterested in the activity, leave it set up for a while after you have completed your picture. He may well try on his own later.

☺   Using an old large coffee tin or similar clean empty container with a lid and a reasonably large base, cut a piece of card to fit the bottom of the container and drip a few blobs of different coloured poster paint onto the card. Encourage your child to add six marbles, one at time, and to listen to the marbles drop into the container (this is where a tin gives the most pleasing sound). Use lots of 'ready…steady…go!' encouragement. Replace the lid and let your child shake the container vigorously. Take off the lid and remove the card – the marbles will have dragged the paint over the card in an attractive random pattern. Try different colour/card combinations.

In summer, outdoor creative sessions can be very messy and enjoyable! Obviously be aware if your child has sensitivities to bright light, heat, and sounds outside and only attempt sessions outdoors when he is relaxed and comfortable.

Try the following activities outside:

☺   Flick paint onto paper from brushes or string. This activity can be used to great effect to increase anticipation and motivation to communicate. Demonstrate the activity a few times first yourself. Use gasps of delight to build up anticipation before you flick the paint. Look at your child and wait for him to make a communicative exchange (eye contact, a purposeful sound etc.) before saying, 'Yes?…Lets do it again!…Wheeeee…!'. Try to make your child aware that you have acted on his request – that it was his attempt to communicate with you that brought about this enjoyable activity.

☺   Fill a detergent bottle with water and draw big shapes with the stream of water on dry flagstones, or fill the bottle with sand for a different effect. Have a bottle each and copy his shapes first. If he makes a random mark that looks a little like a circle, accept this as a circle and draw one yourself, saying, 'Tom's circle…Mummy's circle!'.

☺   Attach a piece of wallpaper lining to an outside wall and arm your child with a decorator's brush and a bucket of watery paint. You could try putting two large dots at either end of the paper and encouraging him to join the two with a line.

Scissors and glue

Cutting and sticking can be a highly satisfying activity. Again, work around the distractions. If the scissors are just too rewarding as play things in their own right, provide materials ready-cut.

☺   To avoid frustration with scissors, choose good quality safety scissors from a specialist craft shop. Cheap ones often don't cut well or fall apart – frustrating for you, let alone your child! Experiment with different types of scissors (try specialist educational supplies catalogues – see the back of the book for details). Some have springs to make using the scissors easier, and some are designed for left-handed users. Try holding the paper in front of him while he cuts – the tension will make it easier. If your child's co-ordination is simply too awkward, leave cutting for a while and try again after a few months.

☺   For children who are likely to lick glue, ensure you purchase a safety glue. You might want to create a 'no-licking' prompt card to remind your child.

☺   Introduce pictures ripped from old catalogues that you think might appeal to your child's particular interests.

☺   When family photos are developed, try to get an extra set each time that can be used in your craft sessions. Don't forget to take the camera with you out and about on walks, days out, to the shops etc. Your child can re-visit the images and begin to piece together his experiences retrospectively.

☺   Try cutting out the component shapes to make a figure, for example, a head, jumper, trousers, feet, hands. Lay them together at the side of your child's work area. On the card in front of your child, draw a pencil outline of the figure so he knows where to stick each piece without your having to continually direct him. Prompt (physically, by touching his hand and the shape) where necessary, but try to give him time to work it out. Wallpaper sample books are useful for cutting into shapes and sticking down. Also try making a house or car shape. To add further interest provided plastic goggle eyes, pom poms, fur for hair etc.

If your child's concentration span is too short, just stick down one element a day until the figure is complete at the end of the week.

☺ Sprinkle different objects into glue: pasta, buttons, pieces of foil, polystyrene packing, glass nuggets. Use the opportunity for simple turn-taking. Make it fun – handle the objects first, drop them into containers and listen to the sound they make, make them come alive as they 'run' and 'hop' into the glue. Capture your child's attention!

Craft

Painting and free expression is about the *process* of being creative – enjoying the feel of the medium, the actions involved and being able to create a mark or image without too much direction. Craft too is about enjoying the process, but it is also about the satisfaction of having *end products*, about being directed, following instructions and knowing what you are aiming to create at the start of the process. This type of highly structured activity can be both appealing and difficult for children with autism. Being directed takes away the need to think imaginatively. This, coupled with a tangible end result as a motivator, makes craft work very attractive. However, the level of interaction with an adult is high and requires that he concentrates, follows verbal instructions and copies actions, all of which can cause anxiety and distress.

For a specific craft activity, try making a *series* of picture prompts that provides the sequence of what you will be doing and shows the end result. The visual nature of the picture sequence may help your child understand and make sense of what he will be doing – why there is an order to it – as well as anticipate the activity. It is also less direct than lots of verbal instructions.

For example, you could show the sequence of making a mask:

Here are some craft ideas that your child may help you with. Only expect him to join in for short bursts.

☺   Try making a mobile using lots of familiar photos of friends and relatives, or paste them onto a board that can be stuck at the side of your child's bed for him to look at.

☺   If your child likes balloons, let him stick a picture of his choice on one, or he could draw a face and stick hair on a balloon. Give it a name and a personality so that it can 'come to life' when you pat it around the room.

☺   For children who 'paper rip', demonstrate that ripped paper has a practical use as papier mâché! Let your child fill a large (old) pan full of ripped paper, add enough water to cover the paper and simmer on the stove until you have a grey pulp (about 20 minutes). Add a tablespoon of PVA glue and mix well. Allow the mixture to cool and let your child get his hands in. There are many things you can make with the pulp:

  ○   Smear petroleum jelly on the inside of a bowl and line with a layer of pulp. Dry it in the oven (set at its lowest temperature) or in an airing cupboard (it might take a few days). Coat the new bowl with white emulsion paint first and then decorate it with children's poster paints, or stick pictures of sweets (cut from old magazines) on it. Varnish the bowl and use it as his sweetie bowl.

- ○ Make papier mâché 'marbles'. Your child may enjoy the repetition of making lots of little balls. Once they are dried you can use them for turn taking 'throwing' games – see Chapter 8 ('Physical Games and Activities') for game ideas.

- ○ Try sticking the paper marbles onto a piece of card to form letter shapes. Once the glue is dry, hold your child's hand and trace the letter shape, prompting him to sound it out.

- ○ Fill an empty ice-cream tub with a shallow layer of pulp and press your child's hand into it to leave an impression. Then leave the pulp to dry.

☺ Make 'category' boxes of items cut out of magazines: food, houses, people, animals, as well as 'colour' categories of, for example, 'red' things. Using one box at a time, take the pictures out and stick them down onto stiff card with your child or cover a shoe box that can be used to store toys. Label each item as you stick it down. To help your child visually discriminate between each item, don't stick them randomly 'collage' fashion – leave lots of space around each thing and later draw a black border round.

During the course of the day look at things your child is finding difficult to understand or getting anxious or frustrated about because he doesn't have the communication skills to express his fears. Think about ways you can deal with these in all aspects of play, including art and craft. For example, if you are about to take a journey together on a train, aeroplane or even a bus, you might start by looking at a simple book or creating an imaginative play sequence with toys (see Chapter 13). You could then try painting or making a model – you could even use this with music. Make the plane fly to music or sing 'Wheels on the bus' etc. Associate the feel of these things with fun and enjoyment.

Being creative involves more than paint and paper – be creative yourself in your interactions and in your play!

Chapter 13

Creating Imaginative Play Sequences

Dolls' houses, train sets, toy garages, miniature figures, farm/zoo sets, building blocks and a multitude of other children's toys are all designed to stimulate and encourage imagination. When we think about imagination we often relate it to fantasy-style daydreaming; we may even decide that a lack of imagination is not such a disability, allowing focus on the reality of the here and now.

Imagination, however, is much more fundamental to development than simply allowing children to play with a certain type of toy. As children grow and develop, the imagination becomes an extremely useful social tool. It allows us to imagine the thoughts and feeling of others in reaction to our own behaviour. It allows us to imagine an outcome or a series of possible outcomes to a given situation so that we can adjust our behaviour and it allows us to feel empathy and respect for others and these are just the social benefits of imagination!

For example:

> Jack imagines it would be great to play with Dad's laptop while he's out of the room. He imagines different ways he might explore it and how exciting this would be. He then imagines his Dad's reaction to Jack going against his wishes.

Jack imagines what would happen if he broke it and how sad and angry this would make his Dad.

This course of imagination allows Jack to make a considered decision not to take the risk. Using his imagination in this way, Jack could see into the future and imagine a series of possible outcomes. Using imagination also enables us to achieve goals, fulfil dreams and ambitions – it certainly isn't simply about conjuring up nice stories or being artistic.

A core difficulty for children with autism appears to be the inability to imagine. Although this is a natural part of play for non-autistic children, children with autism are often baffled by such play. Even though children with autism may never play with natural fluency, there are ways of encouraging their ability to imagine, which will serve them invaluably in later life.

What type of toys?

Choosing the right type of toy to introduce this style of playing takes a considerable amount of lateral thinking. Your child may already have an interest in cars or train sets but be playing inappropriately (lining up, spinning wheels, stacking, organising etc.). It is tempting to take these toys as a starting point. However, it may be best to leave teaching your child to play appropriately with these until he is ready to allow you to direct some of his play. The objective is not to replace a comforting activity with one which causes confusion and distress, but to introduce another activity which can be used as a starting point to help him play appropriately with a range of toys.

Remember the following in your choice of toys:

- simplicity
- realism
- familiarity.

Simplicity

Start off with only one or two elements from whatever toy category you have chosen to introduce, for example, two or three plastic animals and one building from a farm set or two dolls and a table (an upturned box), two cups and a teapot. Tempting as full play sets are, all those pieces can be overwhelming, confusing and distracting. Once your child has mastered one or two items then you can introduce more.

Realism

Toy manufacturers often try to increase the appeal of their toys by the use of vivid colours/patterns, adding facial features where you wouldn't expect to find them (for example, on cars/teapots) or give items a 'cartoon' feel. With non-autistic children including those with other special needs these things do indeed increase their appeal – they add humour and surprise and stretch eager imaginations. For children with autism it can be confusing to see an item in real life in one format and then changed beyond recognition in a toy replica. Vivid colours and lots of detail add to the sensory overload that children with autism are already trying to de-code. Try to choose realistic items that look very like what they intend to represent, i.e. real-looking vehicles rather than bright coloured ones with faces.

Over recent years manufacturers have also realized that children also often prefer items that look just like their real counterparts and there is now a rising choice of miniature domestic appliances: Hoover washing machines, Dyson vacuums, real-looking kettles/toasters/coffee makers and Bosch power tools. For children with autism, they help to close the gap on the imaginative leap by allowing your child to simply imitate you doing an activity that he understands with an object that he clearly recognizes.

In summary, choose toys your child can relate to (dolls' houses and furniture are also a good choice). As well as items he sees in the home, you may find a set of miniature figures your child knows from the television.

Familiarity

It's amazing that non-autistic children can pick up a rocket, a pirate ship or a castle and simply know how to play appropriately. They can do this because during their short lives they have learnt both directly and incidentally what these things represent – by asking questions, reading stories and looking at pictures they can conjure up scenarios that they *imagine* could take place in these contexts. Children with autism do not have the advantage of such learning – they learn through direct experience of each situation in context. To explain a concept is not enough, as the child's impaired imagination cannot take words and conjure up an image – he needs an *actual* image.

Because of this, familiarity is highly important if your child is going to learn a play sequence with a group of toys. Therefore, if you decide to use a toy zoo, make sure this is after your child has been familiarized with the concept by looking at pictures/going on a trip.

Make the example as simple and concrete as possible. Think about the day – what scenarios (however simple) have you encountered; it might be something like seeing a cat cross the road or passing a building site. Try to refer to events as they happen, describing the scene as you are looking at it in very basic language, for example, 'cat walking', 'digger digging road'. Then use that same description whilst you are playing. Your child may play back the scene in his mind and relate this to what you are doing with his toys. You are trying to create a sense of *meaning* for him by basing his imaginative play on *real* events. Remember the details especially if they are unusual or amusing. If he goes to the park, try a toy playground and figures. Find realistic-looking figures and name them, i.e. 'Mummy and Thomas' etc. Re-enact what you've done in the park – if Thomas fell over, make the doll fall over!

The right environment

In everyday life, non-autistic people have little difficulty filtering out information they don't need and processing only the information relevant to the task. It helps us focus on the person talking to us in a room full of chatting people; it means we are able to read or write with the TV on or music in the background. We can walk and negotiate our way around objects as well as talking and listening. We not only process a vast amount of information coming into our senses, we also have the ability to unconsciously ignore a great deal of superfluous information and block out sensations that distract us. As I sit here I am vaguely aware of the hum of the computer, the hardness of the wooden chair I'm sitting on, traffic noise outside and the smell of fresh coffee from downstairs; however, none of these sensations are competing with my attention to the screen in front of me – my visual input. Now imagine how difficult it would be to concentrate if you were unable to shut things out. Children with autism often have distractions that we might only be dimly aware of – itchy clothing, sun pouring in through open curtains, the hum of refrigerators, fluorescent lights. Not only might these sensations be annoying and impeding your child's ability to focus on one thing, they may also be unpleasant to the point of being painful.

The reason for creating such a detailed picture of sensory processing difficulties is to draw your attention to your child in his environment every time you attempt an activity with him. Try to be aware of things that might be problematic for him other than the obvious background TV noise. Do a brief check of the senses –

check for noise that can be reduced, for light that might be too bright or causing flickering/patterning on the walls, that his clothing is comfortable and not too heavy (autistic children will often just pull off clothing that is bothering them), that there are no strong smells (perfume, coffee, last night's curry). Once you are happy that the environment is right, you can begin. If you would like to read more about the sensory differences between autistic and non-autistic processing, try reading *Autism and Sensing* by Donna Williams.

Getting started

☺   Keep the playing area free of distractions by only getting out the toys you are playing with.

☺   Communicate that it is time to play, for example, 'farm animals', by using a picture card (a line drawing or a photo) to show your child before you bring out the toys. I refer to 'picture prompts' throughout the book, as they are a tried and tested means to help communicate to both verbal and nonverbal children about what is going to happen next. Picture prompts give the child time to mentally prepare for the activity and shift his focus of attention. There is a resource of pictures at the back of this book for you to copy.

☺   Show your child a picture of an activity that can be used as a reward afterwards (see Chapter 4's suggestions for rewards or reinforcers), or use a general 'take a break' card (also detailed in Chapter 4).

☺   Define a specific area to play on – for small toys, try a table top (remove patterned or stark white tablecloths which may be too reflective) – pastel green is a good calming colour. You may wish to use a large piece of card (A2-size) with a line drawn down the centre to show *your* playing area and your *child's* (again avoid stark white card).

☺   For larger toys, play on the floor on a plain carpet or rug (or laminate flooring is ideal). If you have a patterned carpet, try using a plain carpet tile.

☺   Start with two sets of figures/animals/cars – one for you and one for your child. By having your own set to demonstrate how to play, you are not overwhelming your child with directions and encroaching on his space. It gives you the opportunity to introduce new ideas that he can imitate and to copy and expand on what he does. This doesn't mean you have to go out and buy duplicate sets of toys. Children's farm sets, dolls' furniture, building blocks etc. often contain multiples of the same item. Try *making* additional items in two's to support your play, for example, duck ponds can be a piece of oval blue felt material or card, fields can be green squares and dolls' beds and baths can be made from shoe boxes.

Building scripts

It perhaps sounds a little theatrical to talk about 'scripts', but if this is the first time your child is learning to play with such toys he'll need props: stock scenarios that he can fall back on and that help him make sense of what he's doing. The likelihood is that he's already building scripts (verbal and/or physical) for all manner of real everyday scenarios. Occasionally our son will generate a novel way of expressing something but by and large he'll use collections of words put together in the same order (learned phrases) that he's heard before and apply them time and again where he feels they're relevant. As he gets older his ability to do this gets better and more sophisticated. By gathering 'scripts' in this way he is learning to produce the right phrases in response to situations as they arise. In the early days of learning to play, the same phrases were trotted out time and again to the same play activity. It was unspontaneous and not desperately imaginative, but it paid off; it gave his toys meaning and enabled him to play, albeit in a limited way.

Initially scripts should be very short and unfussy, for example: 'Mummy and Thomas in park', 'Thomas on swing', 'Look – a dog!'

Gradually work on adding language and new expressions once your child understands and repeats the scripts (if he is verbal).

☺   Support the scripts visually with a large piece of card which tells the play story sequence. Use line drawings, photos or photocopies from books using three or four pictures that tell a very simple story, for example:

Teddy's tired and yawning.
Teddy puts on pyjamas.
Teddy brushes teeth.
Teddy goes to bed.
Good night, Teddy.

Keep your language very simple to start with.

Individual example: Jonathan

Jonathan, aged three, had received a 'first farm' play set that seemed perfect for him; it was a good size and easy for him to manipulate, the figures were realistic and there was nothing for him to get frustrated with. The problem was his mum simply couldn't get him to look at it. She would set it up on the floor and Jonathan would simply run through it as if it wasn't there. When she thought about it, Jonathan hadn't paid much attention to any of his books with animals in (though he did like books with pictures of tractors!). He could label pig and duck, but his other labels seemed to keep getting lost and he could only echo what his mum said. Jonathan's mum decided to look at what related animal activities Jonathan liked. He loved sitting in his pushchair looking at the ducks and the water when they went to the park, so she decided to take her camera with her on their next trip, and whilst they were there she talked about what was happening in the form of a very simple story that she could remember for later.

They revisited the park a few times over the week and when the photos came back, Jonathan's mum stuck them on a piece of card and wrote the story captions underneath. The story went as follows:

'One day a baby duck sat under a tree. A kind boy threw some bread to the baby duck. All the other ducks rushed to get some, but the little boy gave the biggest piece to the baby duck.'

Jonathan preferred the photos of his real ducks to any of his books about farm animals and ducks. His mum then made up two playing sets, each consisting of:

- ○ two ducks (from the farm set)
- ○ one figure
- ○ a blue felt oval (pond)
- ○ a tree
- ○ pieces of screwed-up tissue paper (bread!).

She placed a large pale green table cloth over the dining room table (she'd found in the past that Jonathan would become distracted by the knots in the wood) and set up the play area as shown below:

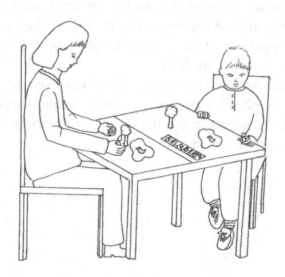

Directly opposite Jonathan she placed the photo script (which she had now memorized). Carefully choosing the best time to play, she held up a picture card (a simple duck outline on a card) to let Jonathan know it was time to play with the toy ducks. Immediately, Jonathan ran into the kitchen demanding a drink (by dragging her arm to the fridge) – this was one of his usual escape tactics. His mum used the opportunity to pick up his drink picture card and pointed to the duck card, saying, 'play first then drink.' Then she sat at the table and began playing as if for her own pleasure, without further directing Jonathan to join her. At first Jonathan ignored her but when he saw his familiar photo story go out on the table it drew him closer. His mum started to tell the same story using the toy ducks. After a while, Jonathan moved in and started to pick up his set of ducks and copied some of his mum's actions. For the first few times they played, Jonathan had the picture story board in front of him. After a while this was no longer necessary. Between them they had found a way to play with something Jonathan previously ignored.

Moving on

After a few sessions where Jonathan copied his mum's actions, his mum tried introducing some variation from the script, or if Jonathan did an action spontaneously she would copy him and give the action words – for example, (when Jonathan knocks the ducks flat) 'Help, we've fallen over!' Jonathan would find this amusing and repeat the action over and over. When he was relaxed and laughing like this his mum felt they were really connecting and sharing space – they were truly playing! If you use a particular character in a variety of scripts (such as a toy figure or small bear), keep him available through the day – pop him in your shirt pocket and spontaneously include him in interactions with your child.

For example, if you find yourself playing a 'pointing at faces' game, bring out the toy and point to *his* eyes, nose, mouth etc. Make the character tickle your child or jump into his lap. A good way to introduce a new character such as a stuffed toy is to pop him in your pocket (as if it were your own). When your child notices and perhaps pulls it out, say, 'You've found spotty dog!', then return the dog to your pocket. Limit your child to a few minutes with it – this will increase his interest in the toy and his motivation to 'want' it.

In summary

- Create an interest that means something to your child – decide on a shared experience (either a regular activity or something that happened and caught your child's attention).

- Create the right environment to play.

- Use only three or four play items each.

- Create a picture story board using photos or drawings and write a simple story (script) underneath.

- Once your child is paying attention, create picture cards or prompts to indicate the activity and a reward/reinforcer that will follow.

- Recreate the story board script. If your child plays randomly, copy him at first until he begins to take notice and then you can start going back to the script. Aim to get him copying you.

- Add some variation and see if your child will copy. At the same time copy any variations *he* makes and give the actions words. Create a sense of shared play by letting him see that how *he* plays has a direct effect on how *you* play.

- With these variations start to add more toys (and take some away if necessary).

- Always use lots of positive reinforcement to motivate your child.

- Don't forget that play scripts can be used in sand pits (teddy at the seaside), at the sink, in the bath etc. However, the controlled atmosphere of indoor table-top play is best to start off with until your child gets the hang of it.

- Try to use your child's special interests, if he has any –
  but be wary of them becoming too distracting.

- Keep play short at first – two to three minutes is long
  enough. The quality of your child's interaction with you
  is far more important than how long you can hold his
  attention. Be patient – judge how ready your child is to
  tackle this type of activity. If you feel it is beyond him
  now, concentrate on the simpler interactive play
  activities detailed in other chapters such as Chapter 6
  ('Music') and Chapter 8 ('Physical Games and
  Activities'). Come back to imaginative play sequences
  when you feel you might elicit a response.

- Introduce play characters throughout the day by being
  spontaneous and responsive to your child's interactions
  with you. Be aware that limiting his access to a toy
  which appears to be interesting and important to *you*
  will build on and increase his motivation to play with it.

More suggestions

☺   Teddies' tea party/picnic.

☺   Car stopping at a zebra crossing for people to cross the
road (use white paper with black stripes drawn on for the
crossing).

☺   Doll putting rubbish in bin (use plastic cups for bins).

☺   Doll getting ready for bed (brush hair/teeth, wash).

☺   Dolls' house figure washes toy car.

☺   Elephants/rhinos/penguins washing at the zoo (use a
small dish of water each and plastic zoo models).

I can't draw!

The prospect of drawing 'story boards' and picture prompts might seem a little daunting if you don't consider yourself to be artistic. However, you really only need to do very simple 'stick people' drawings in different poses. Then add line drawings for tables, chairs etc. For example:

If you can take the time to master a few rudimentary line drawings it will be very useful for all manner of ways of communicating with your child – from picture diaries to help with speech and language.

If you are really struggling, then fall back on the camera – set up the toys in the sequence of the script and take a series of three or four photos. A basic instant camera is a good investment. The film is relatively expensive, but it will probably take you a month to use up a normal film and develop it. If you have a PC, perhaps consider a digital camera or try clip art packages for a variety of images.

Problems

If your child resists even looking at what's going on, let alone taking part, try the following:

- Leave the story board out (stuck to the fridge/door) for a few days and find as many opportunities as you can to look at it. If it still doesn't interest him, try another story.

- Fall back on your attention-grabbing tricks (see Chapter 2).

- Check whether your reward card is motivating enough – it might need changing.

- Make a video of yourself playing, for him to imitate (see Chapter 11).

- Check your timing is right and that he isn't over-tired, unwell, hungry, needing the toilet.

- Is there a special interest that you can work into the script?

- Try putting all the items into two lidded cardboard boxes (shoe boxes are ideal) or fancy gift boxes – those covered with holographic paper are appealing. See if your child will watch and copy you empty out the items and put them back in, one by one. This will get him used to handling them and watching you whilst performing a reasonably easy task. You can then use this as a starting point.

This seems like so much effort!

It does indeed, but remember you're only putting in place the very first building blocks of imaginative play, giving your child a set of actions (or actions and words if he is verbal) that are meaningful to him and you. Despite his communicative and imaginative disabilities, from these tentative beginnings the aim is to increase his ability to generalize – to transfer one script to a different set of toys and to change outcomes. He may never play with the grace and fluency of an average child his age but having some way of playing, no matter how limited, means:

- he will fit in better at nursery/play group by understanding how to relate to toys

- he will not be totally lost in other people's houses where there are different toys available to him

- you will have a way to show him how certain *actions* can cause *reactions* in others (for example, if you push or hurt another child, he or she will be sad and cry).

- you will have a means to re-enact and reinforce his understanding of events that have happened in the past

- you will have a tool to warn him of future events or of surprise things that might happen during a normal routine.

Creating imaginative scenarios with toys is one of the most demanding play tasks for children with autism, but like all playing and learning, there is a way to break it down into simple actions that can be related to, copied and expanded.

Chapter 14

Introducing Books and Reading

The problems

Announce to a non-autistic child, 'Let's look at a book' and provided they're not embroiled in something already demanding their attention, you will have them riveted to your side and hanging on to your every word within minutes. Reading together provides lots of opportunities to explore new concepts, images and language. It brings one-to-one attention and a physical closeness and security that children crave. Children with autism find all of this a problem for the following reasons:

- Sitting down and listening to a book means a break from whatever activity your child is currently doing – even if this seems meaningless, like balancing string or flicking paper. Your child's preferred activity takes all of his attention and concentration as it removes him from the real world, which he finds painful and confusing. It is probably a highly pleasurable experience to have to break from.

- A book is a potential source of change – new words to listen to, new images to look at and to try to interpret – all of which are a very real cause of anxiety. All of your child's energy goes into recreating sameness; the very essence of picking up a new book is to delve into something unfamiliar, to stimulate the senses with new ideas. This is a very frightening thought for him.

- Most children with autism have sensory problems to varying degrees; auditory processing problems may make actually listening to your voice highly uncomfortable and sensory defensiveness may make the physical closeness (especially if this involves you putting an arm around him) an equally unpleasant experience.

- Reading and looking at books together is very much a shared experience. Your child probably resists allowing you into his space for many such joint experiences.

- There may be external interfering factors such as background noise – not just the obvious TV and radio but fluorescent lights, heaters, traffic noise etc. They may already be bombarding your child's auditory senses, making focusing on your voice even more difficult.

It's going to take a lot of perseverance if you are going to encourage your child to not only physically allow you to share a book, but to actually enjoy it. Your efforts, however, may well be endlessly rewarded by an activity that can be done almost anywhere, with no special equipment and one which you might just enjoy yourself – especially if your child relaxes into a cuddle at the same time!

Starting out – looking at books together

Ask yourself the following questions and try to ascertain what your starting point should be:

- Is your child already showing some interest (no matter how inappropriate) in books? Maybe he likes to carry one around the house, line books in rows, prop books against other objects, rip them up? Watch your child – see what he does when you pick up one of his books and look at it.

- Does he have a *favourite character* who features in books? Does he watch a particular TV programme or listen to a favourite tape?

- Does he have a particular obsession – bin lorries, doors, light switches, vacuum cleaners?

- Does anything make your child laugh? (tickling/ bubbles/balloons/silly sounds?)

All of the above can be used as building blocks in the ways described below. The following cases are *example* illustrations of how observing your child and then using a series of distinct small goals could help you make that first breakthrough into being able to enjoy books.

Individual example: Peter

> Peter, aged three, liked to use books in the same way he liked to use other toys and objects – stacking them in towers or proping them up on their end around the room. Whenever his mum tried to read one, he objected to her touching his 'arrangement' and would pull the book off her knee and throw it on the floor. His mum tried to be enthusiastic by announcing, 'Wow let's read this book. Look, Peter, come and see', but this seemed to stoke Peter's anger to boiling point

until he became so distressed that his mum would replace the book and retreat to a safe distance!

Peter's mum decided to gradually reduce the number of books available for him to stack by removing one or two a night over a period of nights (when Peter was in bed and couldn't see this happening). She then started to introduce a book that hadn't been previously used for stacking (so that Peter wouldn't immediately associate it with this activity). She did this in the following way over a period of three days for two twenty-minute sessions a day:

1. Looking at a book, sitting some distance away, while he carried on with his own activity.

2. Looking at the book, sitting closer to him, while he ate a treat.

3. Reading the book in a quiet tone to herself while Peter moved about the room.

4. Sitting Peter down with a treat and reading the book in a quiet tone.

Peter's mum kept her approach as indirect as possible. She didn't draw attention to what she was doing until she felt Peter was ready to accept this.

Over the next week Peter's mum was able to increase the volume of her voice to normal pitch and to sit increasingly close to Peter (still reading the same book).

Peter's mum made sure she timed the sessions so they didn't clash with Peter being hungry, tired or anxious. She made sure they had plenty of time – unplugged the phone and ensured that background noise was at a minimum. The book she chose was kept strictly for reading and as Peter was left with only a couple of books in his reach he no longer bothered to stack them (though he did continue to stack other objects).

Peter's Mum had now created an acceptance of books that she could work on and had helped her son associate books with their correct use.

Individual example: Fay

Fay, aged seven, loved watching her mum dry her hair with the hairdryer. In fact she loved to touch and stroke anyone's hair, which was often problematic for her parents. Fay had some appropriate play activities but had never developed an interest in books. Her mum had never seen her look at one and even though Fay was very passive and didn't object to her mum reading out loud, she continued to show no interest.

Fay's mum decided to use Fay's obsession with hair to create a picture book for Fay to look at. She collected pictures of hairdryers and stylers out of catalogues and pictures of hairstyles from magazines and pasted them into a scrap book. On the front of the book she stuck a picture of a doll and attached a lock of dolls hair (leaving the ends free for Fay to touch), and pasted a 'flap' over this for added interest. She introduced the book by saying, 'Ooh look…doll hair!' – then lifted the flap. Now Fay's mum had Fay's attention she could spend five minutes playing 'Now you see it, now you don't' using the flap, before turning the pages and labelling each picture – 'brown hair', 'long hair' etc. Fay now had an interest in one book and knew to turn the pages, through it from front to back.

Fay's mum had used a *specific pathway* of interest to create this first building block toward further reading. She had also provided an appropriate release for Fay's strong urge to touch hair.

Ideas

☺   If your child has a favourite TV character, great – you can usually find lots of associated books. Introduce one book at a time (starting with a very simple one) and don't be afraid to use a book that is aimed at a much younger age. The exercise is in creating an interest in the shared activity of looking at books together.

☺   Read the same book quietly to yourself to start, gradually increase the pitch of your voice if your child doesn't appear to object. Only read the book once, but return to it several times throughout the day. If the book contains rhymes, read them in a sing-song voice and keep this consistent each time you read it. If you use a simple 'lift the flap' book, read it as if for your own pleasure, giving a commentary as you go, for example, 'I wonder what's under here?…It's a dog!'. Keep going even if you feel your child is paying no attention – the chances are he *is* noticing you.

☺   Make an 'interest' scrap book – anything that you know your child can't resist looking at.

☺   If your child shows a preference for certain textures, use one of these to cover a carefully chosen book, for example, bubble wrap, silver foil or fur fabric.

☺   Set aside some regular times for reading, but don't be too rigid – follow your child's lead.

☺   Tailor your choice of material to your child's level of receptive language – not to his age.

☺   When you read, do so at a slightly slower speed than normal.

☺   Keep the first book you work on very simple and short. Look for illustrations that aren't fussy and over-detailed. If *you* have to look intently to see what's going on, your child will never work it out!

☺   If it is very difficult to engage your child at the start, try using a reward so that he tolerates you reading the book (if initially this distresses him) or for sitting with you for, say, two pages. For example, if your child likes tickles, then tickle him, reinforcing why by saying, 'Good, reading'. Try starting out with a book about tickles – see the section below on 'specific books to try'.

Moving on – reading for meaning

Non-autistic children learn to apply meaning to what they read with minimal parental input. Sharing books and creating an interest in reading is often established before the school years and is a healthy basis on which the school can build. There is a way of sharing books with children that naturally and effortlessly encourages them to link the pictures to the words, understand and predict story lines and generally take in a great deal of information in one go. The reader/parent usually runs his finger along the words (left to right) to draw attention to the child the significance of the writing and at the same time talks about the pictures, explaining the meaning of new words and leaving gaps for the child to fill in words. The story might be linked to something personal in the child's life, for example, 'Do you remember when you lost *your* favourite teddy?' or the reader may ask him to predict what might happen next. This way of sharing books is a great guideline for creating 'meaning' to the words the child is reading.

Problems with reading for meaning

For children on the autism spectrum, sensory overload and resistance to direct interaction mean that many of the spontaneous and usual ways of encouraging reading can be distracting, meaning-less and ultimately either distressing (if he is bombarded with questions) or boring – 'I don't understand, therefore this is mean-ingless.' On top of this there are problems with ambiguity, literal interpretation, language difficulties and the ability to understand the thoughts, feelings and motivations of others.

Another hurdle on the path to developing literacy in children with autism is, in the first instance, gaining 'access' in order to create an interest in books. Using the ideas detailed earlier in the chapter, spend as long as it takes to encourage your child to feel comfortable and relaxed when looking at a book in your presence before you attempt to increase his understanding of the content.

If you have got your child to the stage where he will let you read a very simple book to him, enjoys it and appears to listen to and understand the story, has favourite stories and is working on pointing, then there is no reason why you shouldn't start develop-ing comprehension and early reading skills. It may take weeks, months or even years of consistent hard work, but once you've found a pathway to gain your child's attention and motivation to share looking at a book, you have a very useful vehicle to help him understand all manner of experiences.

Don't be tempted to rush into longer, more elaborate stories just because you have your child's attention. Instead work very gradually on building in some flexibility in order to help your child's comprehension of the story you are reading. Non-autistic children are often happy to let you talk about what you read, for you to ask questions, stopping and starting the story – they adjust to dipping in and out of the text; they are flexible. Children with autism find this difficult – they expect a certain set of words to arise from a familiar book; the very sameness of the words is com-forting and predictable. Once you have one or two books that your child will listen to, you need to test how much flexibility he will allow. Read a line or two and then say, for example, 'Where's bear's nose?', Your child may get agitated that you have deviated from the script or may attempt to simply walk away. Without elaborating further, point to it yourself saying 'there it is' and continue the story.

☺   During the day, re-enact parts of books. For example, if your child stands on tip-toe, say, 'Look – like rabbit in the book'. Then find the book and show him (he may then want you to read it!). Find as many ways as you can to make your child understand that the book is not just a collection of letter sounds strung together but that it tells a story. Your child's imagination needs plenty of help!

☺   Try leaving a few books within your child's reach (although be aware of them being used for other purposes). If he is verbal and likes to recite the whole book, let him – practicing sounds in this way can only be a good thing. But make sure that you also read the book with him and talk about it to increase his understanding. Don't get too excited at your child's new talent. It may sound impressive but is ultimately useless if not supported by understanding.

☺   Once your child is able to recognize and point to objects in the book, move on to verbal labelling, again introduce this slowly following the pace your child sets. At the start you may need to help him by producing the first letter sound or asking him to complete the last word in a sentence, for example, 'We sit on a...'. He may also forget the labels from one day to the next, so keep going back over words that you feel he knows. Support this ability during the day by pointing out the same labels using photos, actual objects drawings etc. Help your child understand that it is not just the 'dog' in a particular book that has the label 'dog', but that they appear in many different shapes and colours.

Your child's problem with generalization includes difficulty with categorizing. Don't expect that just because he knows the label for one picture he can automatically label the real object.

☺   As your child's language moves on, so you can share more and more information about the book. Ask questions such as, 'What's the man doing?' rather than 'What's happening here?'. Being *specific* in this way helps your child choose the right words. Try some simple choices 'Is teddy happy or sad?', 'hot or cold?'. Don't ask too many questions – as soon as your child indicates that he's had enough, move along with the story. To get to this point has taken a lot of effort. By making your child work too hard you run the risk that he will decide book reading simply isn't enjoyable anymore, which would be a tragedy!

If your child is nonverbal then some of this advice may be inappropriate. However, you might want to adapt and experiment with the ideas to increase his receptive language skills and interest in written words.

☺   Gradually work on helping him to point to where you ask. You can either mould his fingers into a point and physically move his hand, or (if this distresses him) touch his hand and then the page, always reinforcing the answer yourself. If your child needs added incentive, provide it. Make him work for his rewards! By doing this you ensure that your child is beginning to understand the content of the book and the language that it uses.

☺   You'll need some extra materials alongside your book to help with labelling. Start with one label at a time (assuming that you are at the level where you have your child's attention, and he is allowing you to point his finger at a picture and label it). Move on to the stage where he is pointing himself. Once he is consistently pointing to a number of objects, try placing alongside the book three pictures of labels he knows (including one of whatever picture you are pointing at in the book), for example, dog and saying, 'Find dog'. Your child is expected to point to or hand you the picture with the dog on – showing that he has learnt to generalize the word from the book illustration to other pictures.

As the parent of a child with limited language you probably have a resource of photos/pictures to help their communication. If not, make creating one a priority. Take photos of everything and anything, look on your computer (clip-art CD Roms are often given away free with computer magazines) and ask your speech and language therapist. (If the material is loaned, photocopy it at your library). The library itself is another excellent resource. Friends and family may also wish to help. If you don't have a computer ask a friend who does to run off, say, 20 pictures of household objects. Ask Grandma for photos of her cat, house, etc. Other people often need you to be specific too. Remember to keep the labelling experience enjoyable for the child, rather than hard work. Try only a couple of labels per reading at first.

☺   Many children and adults with autism think visually, i.e. instead of recalling experiences, events, people with the language inside their head, they see detailed pictures. If your child responds better to pictures/photos than language, then he is probably a visual thinker and learner. Encouraging your young child to recognize letters and words builds in some vital pre-reading skills and puts the structures in place for another method of communication (writing) to support his language.

☺   In your daily reading sessions introduce links between text and pictures, but don't add any more than this, i.e. don't ask your child to point, or ask him questions at the same time as pointing out the text. Do one thing at each session, as switching channels of attention is difficult for your child. He is already listening to your voice and watching your finger – more than that is too much. Go back to a simple book with two–three word sentences, even if your child is currently enjoying longer books. Don't abandon the latter, but after he has looked at his usual length book, pick up the smaller one and draw his attention to the text.

After a few sessions try to encourage your child to run his finger along the words to strengthen his understanding of reading left to right. Each time say, 'Point to words'. If he is unwilling, don't force the issue; touch his finger and use your own finger to point.

☺   Request your child to 'Find start' open the book and announce to him 'The end' at the last page.

☺   During the day, point out signs, text on packets, newspapers etc.

☺   Create a book of photos of significant things/people/ places in your child's life and write the labels underneath. Don't forget to include particular special-interest objects that your child likes. Use this as your first book for linking text to pictures.

Examples might be:

> Alex, Mummy, Daddy, Jane, Fudge the dog, house, television, park.

After a week or so, go over the labels with your child, saying:

> 'This is me' (or 'This is Alex' if your child is having difficulties with pronouns)
> 'This is Mummy'
> 'This is Daddy'
> 'This is my sister Jane'

'This is Fudge the dog'
'This is our house'
'This is the television'
'This is the Park'

☺ Intersperse the sessions with other sessions where you ask questions about the text – but don't try several things at once.

☺ Always be aware of how much information your child is trying to process and how long it takes for him to switch from one task to the other.

☺ During the day try to reinforce your child's understanding of concepts such as 'pretend', 'dream', 'think' as they happen. For example, 'Mummy's *pretending* to cry/be sad etc.' followed by 'Happy now, only *pretending* to be sad'.

Story sequences and consequences

To help your child's understanding of sequences, try making your own simple story sequence. Start with two steps, using a simple drawing on each card. You can also try photocopying a simple story book and arranging the pictures in order, for example:

Use sequences you know your child is familiar with and will understand. You can then add more stages when he is ready.

You can also buy ready-made sequencing cards (see references at the back of the book), which range from simple two-step sequences to quite complicated seven- and eight-step sequences. Don't forget to ask your speech and language therapist for resources such as this.

Goals

Try to have a series of small goals that you and your child can work towards. It helps to write them down – you don't have to spend hours writing 'dear diary' entries; a simple one-line goal at the start of each week on your calendar will suffice. A series of weeks may go something like this:

Week 1
Prepare and introduce a book of favourite things.

Week 2
Encourage Tommy to spend two five-minute sessions a day looking at it with me. (Note: have a reward ready.)

Week 3
Aim to have Tommy sit next to me while I talk about the book.

Week 4
Introduce a real book, sitting at a distance.

and so on...

Your ultimate goal will probably be for example:

Week 12
Aim to read a complete book start to finish and be sure Tommy is able to point to all objects and label six of them himself.

Obviously this is only a guide. Be realistic. Look at what your child is capable of now and don't reach too far too soon. If your child is nonverbal now, it would be foolish to expect him to be labelling objects in three months. Work on pointing, understanding and finding ways for him to communicate to you that he wants to read. Only prepare two–three weeks' goals at a time; seeing three-months' worth stretching ahead will only make you feel despondent at such a huge task. Plus, your child may surprise you and romp through three-weeks' worth in four days, or make much slower progress than you aimed for.

Ten minutes a day may not seem much, but remember you're probably doing this alongside other activities with their own goals. Start with the lowest aim/time – it's easy to increase and much less depressing than finding out you're expecting too much.

Observation, timing and preparation

Watch you child's reaction to his world – his reality is very different to yours. Respect this and use it to gain access. Where books are concerned you need to ask yourself:

- How can I get Charlie to look at a book appropriately?
- How can I get Charlie interested in its contents?

- How can I make the environment as comfortable as possible so that he might contemplate it?

- What might be bothering Charlie about the way I approach it now?

- When would be a good time to approach him?

- When does he seem most receptive/relaxed ?

- How can I communicate to Charlie that it's time to read – do I need a symbol/sign/picture to help him anticipate it?

- Do I need to prepare a special book or source – one that I know might capture his interest?

- Do I need to have a reward ready? If so, what sort (a piece of chocolate, a play with a favourite toy, bubbles, tickles)? How do I communicate that this will come after reading the book?

- What are my goals?

Specific books to try

☺   Many parents have indicated that 'Lift-the-flap' books are a definite hit. They usually have very simple language and a surprise 'reward' in discovering what's underneath.
Try:

> *Dear Zoo* by Rod Campbell (London: Puffin Books, 1985). (There are many titles by this author. All are lift-the-flap, use simple language and are clearly illustrated – not too much detail for your child to process.)
> *Where's Spot?* by Eric Hill (London: Puffin Books, 1983).

Buttercup's Breakfast by Ron Maris (London: Walker Books).

Cars, Boats, Trains and Planes by Jeff Cummins (New York: Orchard Books, 1998).

Tickle Monster by Paul Rodgers (London: Walker Books, 1998).

☺ You can also make your own lift-the-flap book using familiar photos of relatives/friends/household objects. Your child will find it so much easier to relate to an actual photo of the sofa he sits on everyday than to a picture in a book. It takes time and effort to do this but you'll find many ways of using such a valuable resource. For example, once your child has accepted looking at it, you can move on to 'Charlie – go and touch lamp/sofa/chair...' and so on. Many young children with autism (including my son) are fascinated by doors. Instead of plain flaps, make them look like doors – this might increase the book's appeal ten-fold!

☺ Also try books with words that can be said in a 'sing-song' voice or that have lots of simple rhymes.
    Some to try:

Peepo by Allan Ahlberg (London: Puffin Books, 1983).

This is the Bear by Sarah Hayes and Helen Craig (London: Walker Books, 1998) (there is a small series of these beautifully illustrated and rhythmic stories – my son is hooked on all of them).

Ten in the Bed by Penny Dale (London: Walker Books, 1990).

☺ Repetition is comforting and aids understanding. Look at books aimed at very young children. Authors know that babies and toddlers also love repetition and there is a wealth of such books out there. Again, forget the intended age – it doesn't matter that your seven-year-old is looking at a board book aimed at a one-year-old. What matters is that he is looking at it!

Try:

> *The Very Hungry Caterpillar* by Eric Carle (London: Puffin Books, 1974).
>
> *Guess How Much I Love You* by Sam McBratney and Anita Jeram (London: Walker Books, 1987).
>
> *Tickle Tickle* by Helen Oxenbury (London: Walker Books, 1995).
>
> *We're Going on a Bear Hunt* by Michael Rosen and Helen Oxenbury (London: Walker Books, 1993).

☺   Don't forget *humour*. Your child's sense of fun is very much intact – find it and tailor your material. *Dr Seuss* books are a good example. My gut feeling originally was that introducing a book with language that often didn't make sense would not be a good idea for a child who already has a language/communication difficulty. However, many parents report that for some reason these books are often a big hit (again, for my son too, when a relative bought one for him). The one thing they have in common is lots of silly nonsensical rhyming, (maybe to a child with autism they reflect the nonsense he lives in 24 hours a day!). Whatever the reason, they have a formula that just seems to press a button.

Try:

> *The Foot Book* (London: Picture Lions, 1997)
>
> *Mr Brown can Moo* (London: Picture Lions, 1997)
>
> *Wocket in my Pocket* (London: Picture Lions, 1997)
>
> *Dr Seuss's ABC* (London: Picture Lions, 1997)
>
> (All available as board books.)

Also try:

> *The Cat in the Hat* (London: Picture Lions, 1983)
>
> *Fox in Sox* (London: Picture lions, 1980)

The Cat in the Hat Big Flap Book (London: Picture Lions, 1999)

☺   As they get older, many children on the autism spectrum are drawn to the realism of factual books that make few demands on their imagination, or that are focused around their special interests: electricity, water, diggers, buses. Respect this as a pathway to appreciating books and don't discourage it. Eventually they may be used as a reward for maybe reading a short fiction story first. However, don't push. As always, follow their lead.

☺   Finally, it's worth introducing a book that is part of a bigger collection. It makes adding to your child's repertoire so much easier as they are already familiar with the format and some of the anxiety of 'newness' is removed. There are lots about – usually associated with a particular character. Work with a character your child already knows or introduce one gradually, possibly through TV first.

Popular characters

I suspect that the success of the *Teletubbies* is down to its producers actually looking at how toddlers behave and what they like, i.e.:

- Masses of repetition
- Lots of rhymes
- Bright colours
- Simplified language
- Predictable format.

Many of these elements appealed to my son. Even if you feel suspicious of the childish language sounds (like I did) there are ways around this – for example, you can replace 'eh oh' with 'hello' as you read. Again, there is a wealth of associated material to dip into.

Even if my son was older than five I would be tempted to try him with the Teletubbies as I haven't come across anything quite so repetitive, with such simple language – it's definitely worth a try.

Other characters that parents report having gone down well with their youngsters with autism are:

- Fireman Sam
- Postman Pat
- Pingu
- Thomas The Tank Engine
- Mr Men (also a good way of looking at feelings and abstract concepts – grumpy, silly mischief etc.).

My own son took readily to the Letterland series, which has had a very positive impact on his subsequent letter recognition and has a treasure of associated material.

Tape/book packages

You can often find book/tape packages in most book shops, choose a simple one with language and concepts that your child is familiar with (for example, one about a magic porridge pot would mean much less to an child with autism than one about going to the park). Bearing in mind your child's problem with imagination coupled with his language disorder, it's not surprising that the concept 'magic' probably means very little to him. This does not mean that imaginative stories are out of bounds, but keep them simple. Your child knows what a teddy is and knows what eating is – so a teddy bears' picnic is something he may well understand. You can enhance this understanding by enacting a picnic with his bears (real food would provide realism and incentive!).

☺   Once you've found a suitable tape/book package introduce the tape first (indirectly) – play it quietly in the background while your child is already engaged in something they enjoy (eating, bathing, repetitive activity). Don't let your child see you put it on – this may cause anxiety that something is about to happen. Gradually accustom the child to the tape first until he begins to indicate that he is listening/registering it being on (this will take as long as your child needs!) Use this as the first building block to go on to introduce the book.

☺   Try nursery rhyme tape/books first – audio stories tend to be quite long, with elaborate language, so wait till your child has a good grasp of language before using these. There are some song tapes with a mixture of very short stories and rhymes.

Try:

> *My Busy Book* by Chris Riddell (London: Walker Books, 1998)
>
> *Nursery Rhyme Song Book and Tape Pack* by C. Hooper (London: Usbourne Publishing Ltd., 1997).

Better still, *tape yourself* reading your carefully selected books/rhymes!

Early literacy

Why include literacy in a book about play? Learning to read and write doesn't have to be about sitting in classrooms or at tables quietly churning out work. It can be about running across the garden to collect a letter, throwing words into baskets, running round the park to form an invisible letter shape and generally about having lots of noisy, physical fun – playing!

Word recognition

Word recognition is something children with autism often find quite easy – letter shapes are constant and predictable and form patterns when put together that always say the same thing, for example, 'c' followed by 'a' followed by 't' always says 'cat'. I imagine written words can be a source of predictable comfort in a world where everything is very unpredictable.

First, try the following ideas to increase your child's ability to recognize written letters. Remember to vary the way they are presented to make your child aware that a handwritten letter says the same as a typed one, or one in a different typeface.

☺   On large (A4) pieces of card, write single (lower case) letters and spread them about the room. Play a 'ready, steady…go' game, for example, 'fetch me the letter "b", ready, steady…go!' Remember to reward with tickles etc. Keep the game short (only three or four requests) to keep up interest. This game isn't restricted to indoors – move it outdoors for even more scope to run around. You can hang letters off trees, hide them in sand pits, stick them to garden canes like flowers etc. A second adult can be very useful to either give the instruction or run with your child and prompt him to choose. This is also a good game for siblings to play, either for the child with autism to watch or to participate in.

☺   Practise making letters out of play dough or cooking dough, or use an obsessional item (if it's possible) to form letters, for example, pieces of string, favourite blanket.

☺   Write letters on the dry ground outside with water in a squirty bottle.

☺   Carve letters into sand – children with autism find the speed and immediacy of this type of activity more interesting than a longer activity that demands more concentration. If, however, your child sits for a long time lining things up, for example, try sitting alongside him lining up your own set of items (cars/dominoes/marbles) into letter shapes.

☺   Make potato letter prints – you don't have to carve the letter into the potato; make a simple circle or square shape and use lots of marks to make the letter (see illustration below). To guide your child, put marks on the paper for your him to print over, or work 'hand over hand', gently guiding where he puts the print. For further ideas on working with paint, see Chapter 12.

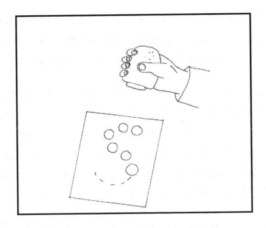

☺   In the garden or park, try playing follow-the-leader in the shape of a big letter – better still, chalk a large letter on the ground and run around its lines. All the time, enforce the letter sound by singing or saying it as you move around it, using the phonic sound of the letter at first.

Once your child can recognise all the letters of the alphabet, start putting them together to make words. All the above ideas can be used with whole words. In addition you can then try the following:

☺   Write written labels for household objects and stick them up with blue tack around the house.

☺   Play fetch games for 'Fetch me the word that says lamp' (your child is initially given lots of visual help by the item it's stuck to). Remember to build in lots of encouragement and rewards and to make this a fun activity.

☺   Try making an assault course, for example, crawl through a tunnel, balance on the cushion, jump to the beanbag and collect the word 'dog' (stuck to the soft-toy dog). If you join in this yourself, you'll generate more interest!

☺   After a few attempts, remove the words from their associated items and try the game again in reverse, i.e. asking your child to stick the label on the correct object.

☺   Make a post-box out of a shoe box and play a posting game. Draw a picture of the word on the reverse of the card so that your child can find the word himself by looking at the picture – too much direction and 'help' from you can be very off-putting. Make a mental note of the ones he needs to check the picture for first and practice these more often.

☺   If your child is not ready to allow such a high level of direction, label items anyway. After a few days, try taking off a label and putting it where your child can come across it – he'll probably return it to its rightful place! Children with autism often take in information that parents have no idea about.

☺   Always be aware of using the learning potential of special interest activities.

Individual example: Lewis

From a very early age, Lewis had been completely fascinated by the washing machine. His parents had successfully used this interest to help him play by providing a toy machine with a handle that turned the drum inside around. They encouraged him to peg out the clothes and iron them and even though this type of play was very repetitive, Lewis was engaged, happy and reasonably receptive, which was an improvement on simply staring at the real machine for hours at a time. Lewis didn't show much interest in letters at the age of four, even though he was able and verbal. He simply refused to join in activities such as looking at alphabet books.

His mum decided to introduce letters into the washing machine play. Taking a number of small white square handkerchiefs, she wrote letters on them in permanent marker pen and produced them as washing. At first Lewis took no notice of the letters but his Mum watched as he played and when he held up the handkerchiefs to peg them out or spread them out and looked at the letters she would sit next to him and say the letter sounds to him. After a few days Lewis had started remembering them and would announce the letters as they went into the machine. Moving on was easy. They started to peg three letter words onto his toy washing line, or would play 'ready, steady…go' games with his mum saying, 'Fetch the letter 'w'…ready…steady…go!'. In the space of a few weeks, Lewis went from not knowing any letter sounds to recognizing all 26 letters consistently.

Activities to develop language understanding

Verbs

In many respects verbs are the bread and butter of language. They tell us what something is *doing*, for example, 'Teddy is *sitting/jumping/ sleeping*'. Ensure your child understands what the word means first by carrying out the action yourself or making a toy do it – remember glove puppets and toys act as a 'third party' and remove some of the anxiety surrounding direct approaches. Encourage your child to act out the action with you. Use songs and action rhymes to support this type of learning. You can try the previous exercises for recognizing verbs, as well as the following:

☺   Collect a word in a 'ready, steady…go' game and act out the action. Start with very simple ones first. You might try 'jumping' to collect the word 'jump' or 'hopping' to collect the word 'hop'.

- sit
- jump
- walk
- hop

Collect a resource of simple pictures showing actions. Either take them from magazines or, if you're feeling brave, draw some yourself. See the back of the book for suppliers of picture cards.

You can use lots of copies of these in the following ways:

☺   Matching written words to the picture of the action. Again, try to give this activity lots of meaningful fun – make the words and pictures as big as possible, act them out, use lots of rewards. If, for example, you're playing outside, match one item followed by using the slide.

Adjectives

☺   The matching game can be adapted to work with *adjectives*. Make a board and stick material of various textures on it (fur, silver foil, sandpaper, cotton wool etc.). Use a word to describe each material and stick with it, for example, furry, shiny, rough, soft. Write the word under each texture. Collect a selection of items that are distinctly one texture (soft toy, spoon, bark, pom pom) and play matching the item to the board.

☺   Also try feeling the items inside a bag (pillow case) and describing how they feel. To do this you might have to sit with your child next to you and put your hands in together and hold the same object. If your child won't tolerate this level of contact, let him pull items out on his own whilst you label them verbally and with a written label. Use the game to observe which textures your child is drawn to and which he finds aversive. Unusually, he might like the stone or spoon against his cheek and hate the cotton wool. Games like these help you understand your own child more and put you in a prime position to help them.

Prepositions

☺   All physical activity games can be used to reinforce understanding of prepositions (on, in, under, in front, behind etc.). My own son could not recognize what 'under' looked like as a drawing (pictures of teddy under the table etc.) for months. When I took his hand and sat under the table, crawled under the slide and made a bridge with my legs for him to crawl under, he had mastered the concept within two days! After this we could move on to pointing to pictures and finally matching the words to pictures.

Pronouns

Many children with autism find pronouns (I, you, he, she etc.) difficult to get to grips with and often reverse them making understanding their requests tricky. For a year my son would say, 'You want biscuit' instead of 'I' and was often frustrated by the reply 'No thanks'! Try to help your child gain a sense of 'self' by using lots of mirror play and talking about what you have/are etc. For example:

☺   Hold a mirror each or sit side by side looking at the same mirror and say, 'Mummy has long hair, Janine has short hair; Mummy has blue eyes, Janine has blue eyes' etc. Intersperse this by using pronouns – 'I have glasses, you don't have glasses'.

Using stickers, put them on each other's face. See if your child will follow the instruction, 'Put a sticker on Mummy's nose, put a sticker on Janine's chin'.

☺   Play 'I can see' games, looking out of the window. Take turns to say 'I can see a…tree…house' etc.

☺   Using cards with a picture on both sides, hold them up in front of your child and say, 'I can see a ball'. Your child responds with 'I can see a dog'. This type of activity also supports his understanding that we do not all see the same things at the same time – we have different perspectives. You can easily create this activity by using flashcard-size pieces of card with magazine pictures pasted on each side.

Please note that the chapters on using puzzles (Chapter 5) and music (Chapter 6) include skills such as matching, being aware of difference, listening, memory and concentration games, and rhyming – all valuable pre-reading skills.

Finally

Parents of children with autism are tackling big issues of behaviour, anxiety and communication on such a daily basis that learning to read might seem like an elusive and unrealistic goal. For some children this may be the case and concentration should be focused on joint play activities and communication. However, just because a child has limited communication skills, provided their receptive language is at a moderately good level, then understanding the written word and more importantly being able to communicate on paper (or computer) could be the most invaluable skill they ever learn. The Internet has opened up a whole community, where people can get together and communicate in a way that was never possible before. There are also some amazing pieces of self-expression to be found from people who are practically non-verbal. There is still a great deal about the autistic condition that is simply not understood. On this basis, an open mind about your child's abilities rather than disabilities means exposing him to as many learning opportunities within the realms of realistic everyday living as possible.

Chapter 15

Problems, Frustrations and Tantrums – Making Play Enjoyable

Deal with your own frustration first!

As parents, we often feel that the outside world shares a common view that how our children are is a product of their engagements and interactions with us, that they come into the world with a blank programmable brain that we fill with love and attention and encouragement to create an embodiment of the qualities we desire in a child. This is not the situation for any child. Of course, the environment they are part of has a significant impact on who they become (ask any adult who suffered an abusive childhood), but working alongside this factor is their own unique biological make-up – a personality or disposition that is reflected in everything they say and do.

For a child with autism there is a third factor – a set of parameters that nature has put upon the brain that interferes with their whole experience of being human. Even though we have the knowledge that these parameters are caused by a biological (and not a psychological) problem with the brain, the invisibility of such a disability can cause the parent a great deal of stress especially in the early years of trying to understand your child as a 'child with autism'. We find ourselves looking at a physically 'normal' (and often very attractive) child acting bizarrely and inappropriately in a public space and want to scream, 'Just behave normally for once!'. I recall our little boy dropping to the floor and sniffing the ground in a shop simply because he was asked, 'What's your name?'. Luckily the shop keeper smiled and said, 'They're all a bit mad at that age!'. She was probably right. We could get away with an awful lot in the toddler years – screaming, tantrums. It was easier to put a three-year-old over my shoulder and haul him back to the car than it ever will be with a ten year old! There is no denying that a child of any age with autism heightens the stress level within his home – anyone who would deny this is being unrealistic.

Before we can deal with our child's stress and frustration we must first tackle our own and appreciate that there are some things we are not going to be able to do:

- We cannot shout, scream or cajole the autism out of our child.

- We cannot make him 'join us back in our world' by forcing our attention and demanding his response.

- We cannot allow our feelings of hurt and anger to express themselves if our child ignores a toy we were sure he would respond to, or if he rejects our attempts to touch, hold or comfort him.

- We cannot use the same behaviour strategies we might use on a non-autistic child – 'time out', removal of social activities etc. (these would probably be seen as rewards to a child trying to escape involvement).

- Likewise we cannot use the same motivating strategies for good behaviour – 'trips to the cinema', 'bowling' etc. (these would probably feel like punishment).

- We cannot expect that if we devote ourselves for years and years to the 'recovery' of our child that he will grow into an adult without autism. No matter how well he can function, he will always have a brain that works, thinks and processes information differently.

- We cannot constantly compare our child to both his non-autistic and autistic peers – his experience is unique.

We *can* however have a positive impact on his developing brain, we can give him coping mechanisms, we can understand his condition to a point where his behaviour no longer fills us with frustration and more importantly we can maximize his potential to learn, interact and experience life. Ultimately, parenting any child is not about what we can reap back for ourselves but about what we can give to our children. If that child is special then what we have to offer him must meet that special need.

In saying that, we cannot leave all our frustrations behind in a single act of conscious selfless will. What we can do is schedule some time for ourselves, for our relationships and for other members of our family. If this means asking for help, then ask; if it means finding solidarity through support groups, then reach out; if it means working out what's important right now and leaving the rest for another year, then do just that. Whatever level of stress and frustration you are having to deal with, your child is dealing with it ten-fold. As adults we have the freedom and maturity to find solutions to such states – your child only has you.

Reducing stress whilst you play

The essence of this book revolves around a number of simple, practical strategies/ideas that you can use to help your child play and interact with a minimum amount of stress. In summary they are:

Understanding

Respect you child's unique experience and inform yourself as best as possible about his condition. Try to be aware of how autism shapes his interactions, his behaviour and his communication. We shouldn't always make excuses for our child but we owe it to him to understand. A child who screams hysterically at the prospect of wearing a different jumper to the one he had on the previous two days is not a '*naughty*' child, he's a *terrified* child, dictated to by a condition that pushes the panic button every time his environment forces him to accept that things around him are constantly changing beyond his control. By trying to work out the meaning behind his behaviour you can find the gentlest ways to modify it. You can also tease apart the normal frustrations and anxieties of childhood from the extreme, odd and confusing manifestations of autism. Some of the most eloquent descriptions of the experience of having autism are written by adults and children who live with the condition themselves; refer to the back of the book for useful reading material.

Structure

Provide your child with a means to make sense of his day. Give him a way to mentally prepare for what will happen next by the use of picture prompts to form a visual diary. As well as the whole day, also structure each activity in turn, break it down into its component tasks (see Chapter 3). Work on achieving one small element of a particular play activity at a time. Use his need for routine to your advantage by introducing regular, short 'learning' sessions at times he expects.

Interaction and communication

Create as many opportunities throughout the day for your child to interact with you in any way he can. Tune into his behaviour and be responsive. Specifically create situations that will motivate him to communicate with you. Make all his attempts at interaction and communication successful for him. For example, if he makes eye contact or any purposeful gesture or noise, reply with 'Again?…Yes, OK. We'll play it again!'. Let him know that communication brings results. Don't just work on verbal communication; explore other ways to support his attempts to communicate. Encourage your child to express his needs and desires through pointing and choosing a picture prompt as well. Don't just 'mind-read' what he may be needing and provide it for him – teach him that *he* can have *control* over his environment by attempting to communicate.

For verbal children, be responsive to everything they say. Even if you don't understand it, reply with 'I don't understand – can you say it again?'. Continue to use visual supports to increase your child's understanding and to help him have control over the events of the day. Visual supports can also help verbal children who repeatedly ask the same question (usually about the sequence of events/time) – make timetables and calendars and refer back to them after bouts of questioning.

Indirect learning

Be aware that direct and confrontational interactions with your child may cause him great anxiety. Gently work on his 'in-built' aversion to sharing his experience of his world. Be subtle:

- Use toys and glove puppets as a third party to talk to your child.
- Look at each other in a mirror rather than face to face.

- Use music and rhyming and sing commentaries.

- Engage yourself in an activity as if it were purely for your own pleasure. Play in parallel with your child and respond to his actions and behaviours by imitating them.

- Covet a toy and hold it back from your child to increase his motivation to gain access to it.

Develop a collection of techniques to try when your child strongly resists direct approaches.

Motivation

Use motivators or reinforcers to encourage your child to participate in short bursts of directed play and structured learning. They can be anything from a preferred activity (such as tickling), a social reward (praise, a preferred toy etc.), an obsessional or solitary 'autistic' behaviour or even an edible treat. Ensure he knows exactly why you are letting him have the reward – make a direct picture and/or verbal link between the rewards and the activity he has just completed. Try to link the activity so closely with the enjoyable sensation caused by the reward (for example, tickling), that he is not only motivated to try the task again, but remembers it as being a pleasant experience.

Timing

Be aware of times when your child is receptive, or simply needs to pull back. Watch the triggers that cause him stress and watch for sensations that he cannot communicate that are interfering with his interactions with you. Watch his reactions to certain foods (particularly wheat and dairy products), be aware of how he expresses his tiredness, hunger or discomfort. Plan activity

sessions for his 'best' times of the day and be ready to spontaneously 'go with the flow' if he suddenly seems 'available' to you.

Preparation

Spend some time on an evening working out the general order of
the following day. Set up his visual diary so that he knows what to
expect will happen from the time he rises. Plan the activities so
that you only have to collect a box of items rather than trying to
assemble an activity and watch your child at the same time.

Environment

Create an environment that doesn't overwhelm your child with
choice, noise or colour. Keep play items and their surroundings
clearly defined.

Individuality

Know and appreciate your child for who he is right now rather
than forever pursuing a vision of what he may be able to achieve.
Have goals by all means and open your mind to all the possibilities
that his potential may hold, but never lose sight of the individual
that he is. How he, and only he, deals with a unique experience of
the world. Try to understand and get inside your child's thinking –
don't just pull him down a 'normal' path of learning. Take the time
and effort to find the other pathways and to meet him half-way.

Flexible parenting for rigid kids

Despite the many differences in behaviours and the many places a
child may be on the spectrum, all children with autism wrestle
with issues of explosiveness and frustration. Problems with social
interaction, language processing, anxiety and the 'need to preserve
sameness' are all compounded and you can feel like you are living

with a walking 'time bomb'. Often we may not even notice that we are obstructing part of a routine, or that something is in the 'wrong' place. Other times we may well know what the problem is but have decided that our child's behaviour cannot *always* be accommodated. Once we know why he is behaving in a certain way we can begin to modify our own behaviour, which means revisiting what we expect from our child.

The book *The Explosive Child* by Ross W. Greene visits this subject in a practical and accessible way for parents and is a good starting point for coping with 'explosive' behaviour in children of all ages.

You cannot prevent all tantrums all of the time but you can be instrumental in creating an environment that will reduce their frequency:

- The picture timetable not only helps your child anticipate play activities but reduces his stress at things such as visitors arriving, bed time, etc. – times of the day that may provoke tantrums. Don't forget to take your camera whenever you are out seeing friends, at the doctor's, dentist, optician, shops etc. You can then use these photos on the timetable.

- Keep verbal language as simple as possible. Limit words to the ones that are key to the sentence, for example, 'Shops later'.

- A visual timer (see references at the back of the book) will help your child actually see the passing of time and can be used to give him a sense of how long an activity will last.

- If your child resists a request and starts to go in a downward spiral, ask yourself just how important it is to you that he complies with the request right now. If the matter is a safety issue, then you'll have to stick to your guns and go through the explosion with your child. If it isn't a matter of safety (such as asking him to clear toys away) it may be better to circumnavigate the tantrum and leave such requests to a later date.

- Watch and be aware of situations before they arise. If a certain set of actions, or circumstances has led to an episode of distress and tantrums in the past, try to avoid them in the future before they happen. Modify toys, remove objects (out of your child's sight), be ready armed with the things that will distract and pacify him.

- *Social Stories* by Carol Gray are a good technique to use preceeding and after events that your child doesn't understand or may cause him stress. Social Stories consists of a set of pictures and words that you may read to the child – or the child reads independently. Each Story describes a social situation or concept. The goal of each Social Story is to provide the child with social information that will make the typical responses of others more predicatable and/or logical. Often a Social Story will answer 'wh' questions, describing who, what, when, where and how. Topics are limitless from something simple such as 'wearing clothes' to something more complicated such as 'when to say thank you' or 'visiting the dentist'.

  Social Stories are clearly defined, developed according to specfic crieteria that are consistent with the learning characteristics of children with autistic spectrum disorders. For example, authors only use language at the reader's level of understanding. Parents and professionals frequently write Social Stories to provide information about social concepts and skills that are problematic. Still it is important to note that half of all the Social Stories developed for an individual child should praise those skills a child currently does well, or applaud social concepts the child does understand. This places praise in writing, important to building the child's self-esteem. For more information on social stories see the references at the back of the book. You could try making your own Social Stories using photographs relevant to your child, such as visting grandma. Again only use language at your child's level of understanding and choose topics that are problematic that you can help him understand and deal with before they actually happen.

Reassessing play skills – the need for goals

It's easy to forget 'where we are' with our child developmentally. We can get stuck on trying to encourage just one or two activities or get swamped in hopelessness because our child isn't making much progress in one area. Don't just focus on one field at a time. If your child has poor verbal skills don't feel that he has to concentrate purely on speech before you can move on; look at other ways to support his communication – work at 'sharing space' and behaving appropriately. If you have a little time and energy, try keeping a diary, just a record perhaps of new words or actions, things that have caused distress and things that he particularly enjoyed. Be specific in what you write, for example, 'John sorted the toy animals and toy food into separate boxes correctly today.' Once every six weeks or so, revisit the last section of entries and look at areas that need to be moved on, skills that appear to be developing. Count how many times you have recorded that your child responded appropriately – compare it to the previous six weeks. Appreciate and understand that as he gets older he *is* developing.

Enjoy your child

You might feel that setting up and working through highly structured play activities and finding indirect ways of overcoming our
child's resistance to direction is simply too hard. However, what's
harder – watching your child ignore you and the toys around him
to engage himself in solitary self-stimulating play and seeing him
move from one bout of frustration and distress to the next, or
making some sense of the chaos for him, having the satisfaction
that you are helping his experience of the world by finding some
meaning?

Ultimately, if we can find an 'emotional space' that we can *both*
occupy at the same time, some of the time, through a series of
practical changes to the way we attempt to play and interact, we
can find a way to fill a large portion of our time with him during
the special early years with laughter and responsiveness. Above all,
play is about fun. For all children, fun is the motivating drive
behind play and consequently learning. For your child with
autism, there may always be a 'different quality' to the way he
plays. His fun may not come from the usual routes of imagination
and achievement, but if he can be encouraged to resist and
overcome his internal motivation to avoid in order to interact and
play some of the time then, you will be giving him back a piece of
childhood that his condition might otherwise threaten to take
away.

Bibliography

Alvin, J. and Warwick, A. (1994) *Music Therapy for the Autistic Child.* Oxford: Oxford University Press.

Barnes, P. (ed.) (1995) *Personal, Social and Emotional Development of Children.* London: Blackwell Publishers.

Davalos, S. (1999) *Making Sense of Art.* Kansas: Autism Asperger Publishing Group.

Grandin, T. (1995) *Thinking in Pictures.* New York: Vintage Books.

Grandin, T. (1996) *Emergence Labeled Autistic.* New York: Warner Books.

Gray, C. (2000) *The New Social Story Book.* Texas: Future Horizons Inc.

Greene, R. W. (1998) *The Explosive Child.* New York: Harper Collins Publishers.

Howlin, P., Baron-Cohen, S. and Hadwin, J. (2000) *Teaching Children with Autism to Mind-Read.* Chichester: John Wiley and Sons.

Kranowitz, C.S. (1998) *The Out of Sync Child: Recognizing and Coping with Sensory Integration Dysfunction.* New York: Skylight Press.

Lear, R. (1977) *Play Helps.* Oxford: Butterworth Heinemann.

Matthews, J. and Williams, J. (2000) *The Self-Help Guide for Special Kids and Their Parents.* London: Jessica Kingsley Publishers.

Richman, S. (2001) *Raising a Child with Autism.* London: Jessica Kingsley Publishers.

Schwartz, S. and Heller Miller, J.E. (1996) *The New Language of Toys.* Bethesda: Woodbine House.

Stanton, M. (2000) *Learning to Live with High Functioning Autism.* London: Jessica Kingsley Publishers.

Williams, D. (1996) *Autism: An Inside-Out Approach.* London: Jessica Kingsley Publishers.

Williams, D. (1998) *Autism and Sensing: The Unlost Instinct.* London: Jessica Kingsley Publishers.

Wing, L. (1989) *The Autistic Spectrum: A Guide for Parents and Professionals.* London: Constable and Co. Ltd.

Therapeutic Options / Organizations

The National Autistic Society
393 City Road
London EC1V 1NG
Tel: (0)20 7833 2299
E-mail: nas@nas.org.uk
Website: *www.oneworld.org/Autism_uk/*

NAS EarlyBird Programme
NAS EarlyBird Centre
Manvers House
Pioneer Close
Wath-Upon-Dearne
Rotherham
S. Yorkshire S63 7JZ
Tel: +44 (0) 1709 761273
E-mail: earlybird@dial.pipex.com
Website: *www.oneworld.org/autism_uk/nas/earlybi.html*

ABA – Applied Behaviour Analysis
Website: *www.iaba.net/*
   UK contact for ABA Training:
   PEACH (Parents for the Early Intervention in Autistic Children)
   PO Box 10836
   London SW14 9ZN
   UK
   Website: *www.peach.uk.com/*

TEACCH – Treatment and Education of Autistic and Related Communication Handicapped
Division TEACCH
School of Medicine
310 Medical School
Wing E 222H
Chapel Hill, NC 27514
USA
Website: *www.teacch.com*

Autism Independent UK
199/201 Blanford Ave
Kettering
Northants
NN16 9AT
UK
Tel/fax: +44 (0)1536 523274

PECS – Picture Exchange Communication System
Pyramid Educational Consultants UK Ltd
Pavillion House
6 Old Steine
Brighton
BN1 1EJ
UK
Tel : +44 (0)1273 609555
E-mail: Workshops@pecs.org.uk
Websites: *www.pecs-uk.com/*
www.autism-uk.ed.ac.uk/

AIT – Auditory Integration Training
The Listen to Learn Centre
Precise Communication
Milton House
532 City Road
Edgbaston
Birmingham B17 8LN
UK
Tel: +44 (0)121 434 4401
Website: *www.autism.com/ari/aitsummary.html*

The Option Institute's Son-Rise Program
Autism Treatment Center of America
The Son-Rise Program
The Option Institute
2080 Undermountain Road
Sheffield, MA 01257
USA
E-mail: sonrise@option.org
Website: *www.option.org*

Sensory Integration Therapy
Sensory Integration Network
UK and Ireland
26 Leopardstown Grove
Blackrock
Co. Dublin
Ireland
Website: *www.iol.ie/~headon/si/*

Dietary Interventions
The Autism Research Unit
School of Health Sciences
University of Sunderland
Sunderland, SE2 7EE
UK

Websites: *www.osiris.sunderland.ac.uk/autism/*
www.gfcfdiet.com/

Recommended Reading

Matthews, J. and Williams, J. (2000) *The Self-Help Guide for Special Kids and Their Parents*. London: Jessica Kingsley Publishers.

Lears, L. and Ritz, K. (1998) *Ian's Walk, A Story about Autism*. Illinois: Albert Whitman & Co.

Harris, S. (1994) *Siblings of Children with Autism: A Guide for Families*. Bethesda: Woodbine House.

Grandin, T. (1995) *Thinking in Pictures*. New York: Vintage Books.

Greene, R.W. (1998) *The Explosive Child*. New York: HarperCollins.

Gray, C. (1994) *Social Stories*. Texas: Future Horizons.

Gary, C. and Leigh-White, A. (2002) *My Social Story Book*. London: Jessica Kingsley Publishers.

Website: *www.autism.org/stories.html*

Williams, D. *Exposure Anxiety: The Invisible Cage*. London: Jessica Kingsley Publishers, in press.

Williams, D. (1996) *Autism: An Inside–Out Approach*. London: Jessica Kingsley Publishers.

Williams, D. (1998) *Autism and Sensing: The Unlost Instinct*. London: Jessica Kingsley Publishers.

Howlin, P., Baron-Cohen, S. and Hadwin, J. (2000) *Teaching Children with Autism to Mind-Read*. Chichester: John Wiley and Sons.

Websites for articles written by adults with autism

www.within.autistics.org/
www.isn.net/~jypsy/ourstory.htm
anu.autistics.org/jane.html

Toys and Suppliers

Chapter 2

Frog in the Box and **Pop-Up Toy** (wooden popping peg men)
by Galt
Educational and Pre-School (UK and overseas)
Tel: 08702 42 44 77 (International +44 161 630 5522)
Website: *www.galt.co.uk*
E-mail: enquiries@galt-education.co.uk

or
Formative Fun (UK toy chain)
Website: *www.formative-fun.com*

Traditional **Jack-in-the-Box**
Golden Days (UK mail order)
Website: *www.goldendays.uk.com*

Bubble Blowing (non-spill containers and battery-operated blowers)
Early Learning Centre (UK toy chain)
Website: *www.elc.co.uk*

or
Dragonfly Toys (suppliers of special needs, toys to USA and Canada)
Website: *www.dragonflytoys.com*

Chapter 4

Sound Shape Sorter (sound puzzle box)
Formative Fun (UK toy chain)
Website: *www.formative-fun.com*

or

Dragonfly Toys (suppliers of special needs toys to USA and Canada)
Website: *www.dragonflytoys.com*

Magnetic Blocks
Hope Education (UK)
Tel: 08702 433 400
Website: *www.hope-education.co.uk*

Domino People Rally
Hope Education (UK)
Tel: 08702 433 400
Website: *www.hope-education.co.uk*

Chapter 5

Hot Dots Power Pen
Educational Insights (USA and UK)
Website: *www.edin.com*

Sound Shape Sorter
Formative Fun (UK toy chain)
Website: *www.formative-fun.com*

Light and Sound Stacking Rings
Early Learning Centre (UK toy chain)
Website: *www.elc.co.uk*

Sparkling Symphony Stacker by Fisher-Price
Amazon (USA and UK)
Website: *www.amazon.com*

Light and Sound Ball by Shelcore
Amazon (USA and UK)
Website: *www.amazon.com*

Picture Cards
Winslow (Education and Special Needs), UK
Tel: 0845 921 1777
E-mail: sales@winslow-cat.com

or

Dragonfly Toys (suppliers of special needs' toys to USA and
Canada)
Website: *www.dragonflytoys.com*

**Threading paddles, threading instruments, sequencing
beads and cards, wooden lacing animals, jumbo wooden
beads**
Hope Education (UK) Tel: 08702 433 400
Website: *www.hope-education.co.uk*

Chapter 6

Sound Lotto
Early Learning Centre (UK toy chain)
Website: *www.elc.co.uk*

or

Dragonfly Toys (suppliers of special needs' toys to USA and
Canada)
Website: *www.dragonflytoys.com*

Chapter 7

Picture Cards – Emotions Why/Because
Winslow (Education and Special Needs) UK
Tel: 0845 921 1777
E-Mail: sales@winslow-cat.com

or

Dragonfly Toys (suppliers of special needs' toys to USA and Canada)
Website: *www.dragonflytoys.com*

Tomy Ball Run, Giant Musical Marble Run, Clown Marble Run
Galt Educational and Pre-School (UK and Overseas)
Tel: 08702 42 44 77 (International +44 161 630 5522)
E-mail: enquiries@galt-education.co.uk

Pull Up Ball Blast by Fisher-Price
Amazon (USA and UK)
Website: *www.amazon.com*

Pound-a-ball
Formative Fun (UK toy chain)
Website: *www.formative-fun.com*

Pounding Step
Hope Education (UK) Tel: 08702 433 400
Website: *www.hope-education.co.uk*

Chapters 7, 10, 11 and 15

Visual Timer
Cicada Educational Equipment Ltd (UK supplier)
Tel: +44 (0)1708 733 388
E-mail: colin@cicada-education.demon.co.uk
For general information and details of USA supplier:
Website: *www.timetimer.com*
E-Mail: jan@timetimer.com

Chapter 8

Outsize Ball
(Gymnic ball from 45–120cm diameter.) Also available: Sensory
Motor Kit, Physio Rolls and Activity Balls. Hope Education (UK)
Tel: 08702 433 400
Website: *www.hope-education.co.uk*

Funky Foot Mat/Funky Keyboard
Early Learning Centre (UK Toy Chain)
Website: *www.elc.co.uk*

Chapter 9

Pavement Chalker
Fisher-Price (UK and USA)
Website: *www.fisher-price.com*

Specialist Tricycle
Hope Education (UK) Tel: 08702 433 400
Website: *www.hope-education.co.uk*

or

Dragonfly Toys (suppliers of special needs' toys to USA and Canada).
Website: *www.dragonflytoys.com*

Chapter 12

Scissors (and many other art/craft materials)
Galt Educational and Pre-School
UK and overseas Tel: 08702 42 44 77
(International +44 161 630 5522)

or

Step by Step
Tel: 0845 300 1089
E-mail: sbs@stpbystp.demon.co.uk

Chapter 14

Sequencing Cards Action Cards
Winslow (Education and Special Needs) UK
Tel: 0845 921 1777
E-mail: sales@winslow-cat.com

Blocks

Dolls

Trains

Cars

Ball

Farm

Balloon

Jigsaw

Doll's House

Hoop

Sand

Tunnel

Bike Swim Workbox

Skittles Draw Music

Slide Read Ball Games

Swing Paint Group Games

Swinging

Ripping

Puppet

Bubbles

Tape/CD

TV/Video

Tickles

Trampoline

Break

Spinning Top

Crisps

Ice Cream

Index